60 From The '60s

60 Players Who Made the 1960s
Baseball's *Real* Golden Age

Carroll Conklin

Bright Stone
Press
Lewis Center, Ohio

60 From The '60s

60 Players Who Made The 1960s
Baseball's *Real* Golden Age

Carroll Conklin

Published by

Bright Stone Press

ISBN-13: 978-1477636671

ISBN-10: 1477636676

Photo Credits –

Front & Back Covers – **Topps Chewing Gum Inc.**

Topps Chewing Gum Inc. – 15, 19, 25, 31, 35, 39, 41, 43, 44, 47, 49, 51, 53, 55, 57, 59, 61, 65, 67, 71, 73, 74, 77, 79, 81, 83, 85, 88, 91, 94, 97, 99, 103, 107, 109, 113, 117, 119, 121, 129, 131, 135, 137, 138, 141, 147, 149, 151, 153, 154, 155, 159, 165, 169, 171, 173, 175, 181, 182, 183, 184, 185, 187, 188, 190

Baseball Digest – 22, 28, 125, 143, 145

The photos used in this book are in the public domain because their sources were published in the United States between 1923 and 1963 with a copyright notice and the copyrights were not renewed. A search of the The United States Copyright Office Online Catalog for records from 1978 to the present revealed no renewals for the above cited photo sources within the required period for filing.

Contents

60 From The '60s

60 From The '60s

60 From The '60s

60 From The '60s

60 From The '60s

Forward

Why Should We Care About the Baseball Stars of the 1960s?

Full disclosure here: I am an unabashed baseball fan, and one who believes that, all things considered, the best baseball ever played took place during the 1960s. I grew up reading that the 1920s were the "Golden Age" of baseball, but I'm just not buying it. You can find Web sites that tout the 1930s, the 1950s, even the 1970s or 1980s as baseball's "golden age."

The 1960s were full of flat-out great players and great performances. And some great stories. Some of those players are celebrated here, with many, many stories to come.

There were plenty of great hitters playing in the 1960s. Willie Mays, Hank Aaron and Roberto Clemente put up awesome numbers throughout the decade, and would fill an All-Star outfield in any era. But they weren't the only sluggers wreaking havoc with major league pitching during the 1960s. The decade was loaded with great hitters: Mickey Mantle, Frank Robinson, Harmon Killebrew, Willie McCovey, Ernie Banks, Lou Brock, Al Kaline, Billy Williams, Carl Yastrzemski. All were Hall of Famers. All were productive year after year and put up fantastic career statistics. And all are profiled here.

Not all the great hitters from the 1960s are Hall of Famers (yet). Whether injuries shortened their careers (as was the case for outstanding hitters such as Tony Oliva and Tony Conigliaro) or they have been unjustly overlooked by the Hall of Fame voters (how else do you explain the exclusion of Vada Pinson, despite his career numbers?), the 1960s showcased great hitters whose accomplishments were all the more impressive when you understand the quality of the pitching they faced.

And the pitching of the 1960s was frequently dazzling. Consider that, since 1920 (and the end of the "dead ball" era), the combined major league earned run average has been under 3.00 only once … in 1968 (2.98). During the 10 seasons of 1960s, the combined major league ERA was under 4.00 every year except 1961 (4.02). As a barometer of that performance, consider that, in 2011, the combined major league ERA was 3.94, the first time it has been less than 4.00 since 1992. During the 1920s, the pitching was also pretty good by ERA standards, as the combined major league ERA was under 4.00 in 3 different seasons (pretty good, but not up to the performance of the 1960s).

My point? Mays, Aaron and company faced outstanding pitching throughout the 1960s, with Hall of Fame starters such as Sandy Koufax, Bob Gibson, Whitey Ford, Warren Spahn, Juan Marichal, Jim Bunning and, at the end of the decade, Tom Seaver. It was also the decade when the reliever was established as an essential pitching specialist, spearheaded by players such as Dick Radatz, Hoyt Wilhelm, Ron Perranoski and Roy Face – all profiled here.

The 1960s saw a number of "sacred" records fall by the wayside. Babe Ruth's single-season home run record and his record for pitching consecutive scoreless innings in World Series play were eclipsed by a pair of Yankees, Roger Maris and Whitey Ford. Ty Cobb's single-season stolen base record, considered untouchable for 4 decades, was broken by Dodger shortstop Maury Wills. Rube Waddell's 60-year record for strikeouts in a season was smashed by Sandy Koufax. Walter Johnson's record for consecutive scoreless innings was topped with 6 consecutive shutouts posted by Don Drysdale.

The 1960s were the last decade when baseball was played without free agents or the designated hitter – two "innovations" during the 1970s that changed the game dramatically and necessarily muddy any statistical comparisons with prior eras. However, the most striking difference between major league baseball in the 1960s and the game during the 1920s and 1930s was the presence of players of color, a diversity that almost certainly elevated the level of play in the 1960s. Imagine baseball in the 1960s *without* Willie Mays, Hank Aaron, Bob Gibson, Juan Marichal, or even a Luis Tiant. Vanilla ball was all there was at the major league level in the 1920s and 30s.

This is not to disparage the skills and performances of the great players of any era. I have no doubt that Lou Gehrig and Lefty Grove would have been great players 40 years later. But I also have no doubt that Sandy Koufax and Roberto Clemente would have been stars in the 1920s, or any decade in between. Whether or not the 1960s were the *real* golden age of baseball, as I believe, the decade did produce players and moments worth remembering and enjoying. The accomplishments of the players profiled here demonstrate a talent and love for the game that deserves recognition, and can never go out of style.

Enjoy the memories!

Carroll Conklin
June 1, 2012

60 From The '60s

60 from the '60s

60 Players Who Made the 1960s Baseball's *Real* Golden Era

Willie Mays

Baseball's Most Likable Power Hitter

The many talents of Willie Mays were on display a full decade before the 1960s began. Yet throughout most of the 1960s, Mays consistently performed at a level few could match.

He hit for average and power. Though perhaps a step slower than when he roamed centerfield in the Polo Grounds (it would be like light losing a step), he still presented a constant threat on the base paths and provided Gold Glove defense in the field despite the unpredictability of the winds whipping through Candlestick Park. But it was his offensive skills that made Mays one of the terrors of the National League throughout the 1960s.

From 1961 through 1965, he belted 226 home runs, more than a third of his 660 career total. In each of those years, he drove in more than 100 runs, and his batting average slipped below .300

Outstanding Feat

On April 30, 1961, Mays blasted four home runs and drove in 8 runs as the Giants routed the Braves 14-4 in County Stadium. He's the only Giant ever to accomplish that feat.

14

only in 1964 (.296). In 1961, he led the National League in runs (129) and runs produced (212). During the Giants' pennant-winning season of 1962, Mays led the majors with 49 home runs and 382 total bases. His 47 home runs in 1964 led the league again.

Yet Mays' most productive season was 1965, when he led the majors in home runs (52), total bases (360), slugging average (.645) and on-base percentage (.399). That performance earned him his second Most Valuable Player Award. He also won 8 Gold Gloves during the 1960s, and 12 in all during his phenomenal career.

Bats: Right **Throws:** Right
Height: 5' 11" **Weight:** 180 lb.

Born: May 6, 1931 in Westfield, AL
Debut: May 25, 1951
Final Game: September 9, 1973
**Inducted into the
Baseball Hall of Fame**: 1979

Did You Know ...

Even though Willie Mays drove in over 1,900 runs during his career, he never won an RBI crown.

Denny McLain

Bad Boy, Great Pitcher

The 1960s was an era of great pitching and great pitchers, especially those who posed a dominant presence on the mound for 3 or more years. Throughout the second half of the 1960s, no pitcher in the American League was more dominant than Denny McLain.

McLain debuted with the Tigers in 1963. His breakout season was 1965, when he went 16-6 with a 2.61 ERA. He won 20 games in 1966 and 17 in 1967. In both of those years, he also led the American League in home runs allowed, a feat he repeated in 1968.

But what McLain is remembered for is not the 31 home runs he gave up in 1968, but the 31 victories he recorded – the first 30-game winner since Dizzy Dean in 1934 and the last to-date. McLain's 31-6 record was achieved with a 1.96 ERA. He led the league in winning percentage (.838), games started (41), complete

---

Outstanding Feat

In a relief appearance against the Red Sox on June15, 1965, McLain struck out 14 batters in 6.2 innings, including the first seven he faced.

16

games (28), and innings pitched (336). He also struck out a career-high 280 batters. In the year of outstanding pitchers in both leagues, McLain collected both the Cy Young award and the Most Valuable Player award for the American League.

He followed up in 1969 with another outstanding season: 24-9 with a 2.84 ERA, again leading the league with 41 starts and 325 innings pitched. At age 25, he had already recorded 114 victories as the decade closed.

Bats: Right   **Throws:** Right
Height: 6' 1"   **Weight:** 185 lb.

Born: March 29, 1944 in Chicago, IL
Debut: September 21, 1963
Final Game: September 12, 1972

He would win only 17 more games, as arm and legal problems brought such a promising career to such an abrupt end. But during the 1960s, only Sandy Koufax and Bob Gibson could match the dominating 5-year performance of the hard-throwing Mr. McLain.

Did You Know ...

Denny McLain was originally signed by the Chicago White Sox.

Roger Maris

Breaking the Legend Barrier

R oger Maris will always be known as the man who broke Babe Ruth's single-season home run record. He was both honored and reviled for that feat. He was also a heck of a ballplayer, and integral to the Yankees' run of five consecutive American League championships in the first half of the 1960s. It is certainly no coincidence that, as Maris's skills faded due to time and injury, the Yankees' fortunes foundered.

Maris was signed by the Cleveland Indians in 1953 and opened the season with the Tribe in 1957, hitting .235 with 14 home runs and 51 RBIs in his rookie year. He was subsequently traded to the Kansas City Athletics in 1958 and to the Yankees following the 1959 season.

In New York pinstripes he blossomed into one of the league's most productive power hitters. A dead-pull hitter, Maris launched 39 home runs in 1960, batting .283 and leading the American

Outstanding Feat

61 homers in a season and back-to-back MVPs? How do you top that?

18

League in RBIs (112) and slugging percentage (.581). He was second in the league in home runs, runs (98) and total bases (290). His performance earned him the American League Most Valuable Player award.

1961 was the year that changed Maris' life – and baseball – forever. His much-chronicled chase of Babe Ruth's 47-year-old single-season home run record brought baseball unprecedented media attention, particularly as fellow teammate – and media darling – Mickey Mantle was pursuing Ruth's record right along with Maris. A late-season illness caused the Mick to miss games that cost him any chance of catching Ruth's ghost, and Mantle finished the year with 54 home runs. Despite the mounting media pressure, as well as verbal and even physical abuse from "fans," including death threats, Maris hit home run #61 on the last day of the season, breaking the unbreakable record and setting one that would stand for 37 years.

Bats: Left   **Throws:** Right

Height: 6' 0"   **Weight:** 204 lb.

Born: September 10, 1934 in Hibbing, MN

Debut: April 16, 1957

Final Game: September 29, 1968

Beyond the home run race, Maris had an outstanding season in 1961. He led the majors in runs (132 – tied with Mantle), RBIs (142) and total bases (366). That performance earned him his second consecutive MVP award.

Maris had another outstanding – though not record-breaking – season in 1962, with 33 home runs and 100 RBIs. Over the next four years, a series of injuries took their toll in diminishing his offensive productivity. He was traded to the St. Louis Cardinals prior to the 1967 season, but never again approached the kind of offensive numbers he put up in his prime as a Yankee. Maris retired after the 1968 season.

How Mickey Mantle Helped Roger Maris Break Babe Ruth's Record

As both were striving to break Babe Ruth's single-season home run record in 1961, the media tried their best to paint Roger Maris and Mickey Mantle as rivals more than teammates. In fact, it seems that both of them got along with each other despite the pressure on them.

In addition, it seems unlikely that Maris would have been able to hit 61 home runs that year if it hadn't been for Mantle. Here's why:

1961 was the year that changed Maris's life – and baseball – forever. His much-chronicled chase of Babe Ruth's 47-year-old home run record brought baseball unprecedented media attention, particularly as Mantle – the media darling in this drama – was pursuing Ruth's record right along with Maris.

A late-season illness caused the Mick to miss games that cost him any chance of catching Ruth's ghost, and Mantle finished the year with 54 home runs.

Despite the media pressure, as well as verbal and even physical abuse from ardent baseball purists who would tolerate "tampering" with the Babe's legend, Maris hit his sixty-first home run on the last day of the season, setting a record that would stand

21

for 37 years (and outlast the asterisk that Commissioner Ford Frick attached to it).

But here's the amazing thing about that season, and Mantle's essential role in Maris' accomplishment. During the season – a second straight MVP campaign for Maris – the Yankee right fielder did not receive a single intentional walk. The most dangerous power hitter of his day was not granted a single free

pass to first base, and the only explanation could be that the guy hitting behind him was Mickey Mantle.

From the pitcher's point of view, pitching to Maris made perfect strategic sense. There would be little to gain by walking Maris and sending him around the bases on a Mantle home run. That would be one run more "expensive" than giving up a home run to Maris.

Maris was consistently allowed to see the kind of pitches he could pull into the right field seats. And Mantle's greatness took on another layer: for that one season at least, Mickey Mantle proved to be nearly as dangerous in the on-deck circle as he was in the batter's box.

Top 5 Right Fielders of the 1960s

1 **Hank Aaron** - From 1960 to 1969, Aaron led the major leagues twice in runs scored and 3 times in RBIs. He hit over .300 in 8 different seasons during the decade, and scored at least 100 runs in 9 out of the 10 years.

2 **Roberto Clemente** - It was during the 1960s that Roberto Clemente emerged as one of the game's premier players. Clemente won his first batting title in 1961 with a .351 average. He repeated as National League batting champion in 1964 (.339), 1965 (.329) and 1967 (.357), when he also led the majors with 209 hits.

3 **Frank Robinson** - In 1961, Robinson batted .323 with 37 home runs and 124 RBIs to win the National League MVP. In 1962, his numbers were even better: 39 home runs, 136 RBIs and a .342 batting average. Following his 1966 trade to the Baltimore Orioles, Robinson won the American League Triple Crown with a .316 batting average, 49 home runs (tops in the majors) and 122 RBIs for his second MVP, the first player to win in both leagues.

4 **Roger Maris** - A dead-pull hitter, Maris launched 39 home runs in 1960, batting .283 and leading the American League in RBIs (112) and slugging percentage (.581). Beyond his 61 home runs in 1961, Maris led the majors in runs (132 – tied with Mantle), RBIs (142) and total bases (366) for his second consecutive MVP.

5 **Al Kaline** – Al Kaline's 20-year career with the Detroit Tigers consisted of steady productivity punctuated with flashes of brilliance. During the 1960s, you could count on Kaline for 20+ home runs, 80+ RBIs and a batting average around .300 year in and year out. His best season during the 1960s came in 1963, when he batted .312 with 27 home runs and 101 RBIs. He won 7 consecutive Gold Gloves from 1961 to 1967, and earned 10 overall.

Bob Gibson

The Cardinals' Strong Right Arm

Hard-throwing, dominating, intimidating: throughout the 1960s, no pitcher was as consistently effective as the Cardinal's Bob Gibson. A power pitcher with great control and a seemingly indestructible arm, Gibson only got better as the decade progressed, and continued his dominance of hitters into the 1970s.

Gibson was called up to the Cardinals in 1959. By 1961, he was a member of the starting rotation, a job he would keep for the next 15 years. The next year he won 15 games with an ERA of 2.81. He had 15 complete games, and he led the majors with 5 shutouts. He also struck out 208 batters that season, and would strike out 200 or more batters in a season 9 times in his career. Gibson posted 18 victories in 1963.

In the Cardinals' championship season of 1964, Gibson won 19 games during the regular season. In the 1964 World Series, he posted two complete game victories, including the deciding seventh game. His performance earned him the Series MVP

Outstanding Feat

In 3 starts during the 1968 World Series against the Detroit Tigers, Bob Gibson struck out a record 35 batters in 27 innings pitched.

24

award. At the end of 1964, Gibson was clearly the Cardinals' ace, and his best years were still ahead of him.

In 1965 and 1966, Gibson won 20 and 21 games, respectively. He was on his way to another 20-victory campaign in 1967 when a Roberto Clemente line drive fractured his leg and sidelined him for the second half of the season. The Cardinals cruised to the National League pennant even without Gibson, who was able to come back and pitch in the World Series against the Boston Red Sox. In Game 1, Gibson struck out 10 batters and allowed only 6 hits en route to a 2-1 victory. He returned in Game 4, giving up only 5 hits in pitching a 6-0 shutout. In the seventh game, he dominated again, taking his third World Series victory by a score of 7-2, with 10 strikeouts and allowing only 3 hits. For the second time in the decade, Gibson was selected as the World Series MVP.

A healthy Bob Gibson no doubt looked forward to pitching a full season in 1968, but he could not have imagined the kind of season he would experience. Gibson went 22-9 with a microscopic 1.12 ERA. He led the league in strikeouts (268) and led the majors in shutouts

Bats: Right   **Throws:** Right
Height: 6' 1"   **Weight:** 195 lb.

Born: November 9, 1935 in Omaha, NE
Debut: April 15, 1959
Final Game: September 3, 1975
Inducted into the
Baseball Hall of Fame: 1981

(13), pitching 28 complete games. He won both the Cy Young and Most Valuable Player awards. In the 1968 World Series against the Detroit Tigers, Gibson won 2 more games. It would be his last World Series appearance.

Gibson closed out the 1960s by going 20-13 in 1969, with an ERA that "ballooned" to 2.18. In his 17-year career, Gibson won 251 games, pitched 56 shutouts and won 9 Gold Gloves. He was elected to the Baseball Hall of Fame in his first year of eligibility.

Did You Know ...

Bob Gibson attended Creighton University on a basketball scholarship and, early in his baseball career, played for the Harlem Globetrotters during the off season.

Gibby's Gotcha

Bob Gibson strikes out 17 Tigers in the 1968 World Series Opener.

Though few might have been around to remember, the 1968 World Series between the Detroit Tigers and the St. Louis Cardinals had much in common with another fall classic 34 years earlier.

The same two teams faced each other in the 1934 Series, with the Cardinals winning in 7 games. And like the 1934 classic, this one featured a 30-game winner in Detroit's Denny McLain. The Gashouse Gang Cardinals of 1934 brought their 30-game winner, Dizzy Dean, who won half of his team's World Series victories, with brother Paul claiming the other 2 St. Louis wins.

In the 1968 Series, the 31-6 McLain won only a single game, being bested twice by the most dominant World Series pitcher of the 1960s, Cardinals right-hander Bob Gibson. Game #1 of the 1968 World Series pitted Gibson against McLain. Both starters worked shutouts through the third inning, and then St. Louis broke the deadlock in the bottom of the fourth. Roger Maris walked to lead off the inning, and after Orlando Cepeda hit a pop foul to Tigers first baseman Norm Cash, McLain walked Cardinals

27

catcher Tim McCarver to put runners at first and second. Mike Shannon singled to left, scoring Maris. Willie Horton bobbled Shannon's line drive to left; the error allowed McCarver to advance to third and left Shannon at second. The next batter, second baseman Julian Javier, singled to right, driving in both McCarver and Shannon.

Now leading 3-0, Gibson would prove to be invincible, as he had been so often in 2 previous World Series. Through the first four innings, Gibson had faced only 13 Detroit batters, allowing 2 singles and striking out 8. In the fifth inning he allowed a walk to catcher Bill Freehan, but struck out Don Wert looking. In the sixth

inning, Gibson gave up a single to Dick McAuliffe and a double to Al Kaline, but recorded 2 more strikeouts to end the inning without allowing the Tigers to score. He retired the Tigers in order in the seventh inning (with 2 more strikeouts).

St. Louis had increased the lead with a Lou Brock solo home run in its half of the seventh inning, and Gibson shut down the Tigers in order again in the bottom of the eighth (1 more strikeout). Mickey Stanley opened the top of the ninth with a single to center, the Tigers' fifth – and last – hit of the game. Working from the stretch, Gibson struck out Kaline, Cash and Horton to end the game.

Gibson finished with 17 strikeouts and only 1 walk. He would come back in 5 days to beat the Tigers and McLain again, this time 10-1, pitching another 5-hitter and striking out 10.

It would be hard to imagine any pitcher being more dominant in the World Series than Gibson was in his first 2 appearances in the 1968 Series: 2-0 with a 0.50 ERA and 27 strikeouts in 18 innings.

Top 5 Pitching Performances of the 1960s

1 **Sandy Koufax: Perfect When He Had To Be** - Koufax tossed 4 no-hitters during the 1960s. On September 9, 1965, Koufax retired all 27 of the Chicago Cubs he faced, 14 by strikeouts, as the Los Angeles Dodgers beat the Cubs 1-0. The losing pitcher, Bob Hendley, allowed only one hit and two base runners, losing on an unearned run. Perfect, that night, beat nearly perfect.

2 **Catfish Hunter's One-Man Show** - It would be hard to imagine any player – at any position – having a more "perfect" day than the one Hunter had on May 8, 1968. He drove in 3 of the Oakland A's 4 runs, including the game-winning run. He also struck out 11 Twins in route to pitching the first regular season perfect game in the American League in 46 years.

3 **Bob Gibson's Record World Series Whiffs** - Gibson had a pretty good year in 1968 (22-9, 1.12 ERA, 13 shutouts, MVP) But he pitched even better in the World Series against the Detroit Tigers. In 3 starts, Gibby struck out 35 batters in 27 innings, including a record 17 Tigers he fanned in Game 1.

4 **Denny McLain's 30-Win Season** - McLain's 31-6 record in 1968 was achieved with a 1.96 ERA. He led the league in winning percentage (.838), games started (41), complete games (28), and innings pitched (336). He also struck out a career-high 280 batters, and collected both the Cy Young award and the Most Valuable Player award for the American League.

5 **Dean Chance's Shutout Show** - Dean Chance was the American League's most dominant pitcher in 1964, his Cy Young season. His 20-9 record included leading the league in innings pitched (278) and complete games (15), with the majors' best ERA at 1.65. He also hurled 11 shutouts, six by 1-0 scores.

Frank Robinson

Most Valuable in Either League

The level of Frank Robinson's talent was matched only by the intensity of his competitive nature.

Whether as a player, manager or front-office executive, Frank Robinson was a winner who would settle for nothing less. His skills, matched with that determination, made him a consistent winner – if not always the most personable guy in the clubhouse – throughout his career.

Robinson came to the major leagues through the Cincinnati Reds organization, batting .290 as a rookie in 1956 and leading the National League in runs scored with 122. He also led the league in hit-by-pitches (20), a dubious honor he would repeat 6 more times in his 21-season career.

By the beginning of the 1960s, Robinson was already a star. In 1961, he batted .323 with 37 home runs and 124 RBIs as the

Outstanding Feat

Frank Robinson's Game 4 solo home run – combined with Dave McNally's shutout pitching – clinched the Orioles' World Series sweep of the Los Angeles Dodgers in 1966.

offensive leader for the National League champion Cincinnati Reds. For that performance, he was named National League Most Valuable Player for 1961.

In 1962, his offensive numbers were even better: 39 home runs and 136 RBIs and a .342 batting average. He also led the major leagues in runs (134), doubles (51), and slugging percentage (.624) that year. But his offensive production dropped slightly over the next three years, and the Reds shipped Robinson to the Baltimore Orioles for pitcher Milt Pappas and two other players.

It was probably the best trade Baltimore ever made. Robinson had a monster year in 1966, winning the American League Triple Crown with a .316 batting average, 49 home runs (tops in the majors) and 122 RBIs. Robinson also led the majors in runs scored (122), total bases (367) and slugging percentage (.637). He was named American League Most Valuable Player for 1966, the first player to win that award in both leagues.

Bats: Right **Throws:** Right
Height: 6' 1" **Weight:** 195 lb.

Born: August 31, 1935 in Beaumont, TX
Debut: April 17, 1956
Final Game: September 18, 1976
Inducted into the
Baseball Hall of Fame: 1982

Due to injuries, Robinson's numbers declined in 1967 and 1968. But he had another outstanding season for Baltimore in 1969, batting .308 with 32 homers and 100 RBIs.

A Hall of Famer with 586 career home runs and over 1800 RBIs, Robinson closed out his playing career with the Cleveland Indians, where he was also the first African-American to manage a Major League team.

Did You Know ...

Among right-handed hitters, only Hank Aaron and Willie Mays have more career extra-base hits than Frank Robinson.

Top 5 Trades of the 1960s

1 **Baltimore Orioles Acquire Frank Robinson** – From 1962-1965, Robinson hit for a combined .303 with an average of 30 home runs and 109 RBIs per season. Yet the Reds felt that Robbie was on the downside of his career and dealt him to the Baltimore Orioles. All the Orioles got in return was the 1966 Triple Crown winner and American League MVP – the first player to win an MVP in each league – and a World Series championship in 1966.

2 **St. Louis Cardinals Acquire Lou Brock** – This was probably the most lopsided trade of the 1960s. (After all, Milt Pappas was 30-29 in 2-plus seasons for the Reds. The Cardinals dealt 2 pitchers who won a total of 8 games for the Cubs, while Brock led the Cards to the World Series.) In 103 games, he hit .348 and scored 84 runs, with 12 home runs, 44 RBIs and 33 stolen bases.

3 **Chicago Cubs Acquire Ferguson Jenkins** – It looked like a steal for the Phillies, who got 2 proven major league starters, Larry Jackson and Bob Buhl, who combined for 47-53 for the Phillies. Jenkins won 20 or more games for the Cubs in 6 straight seasons on his way to winning 284 in a Hall of Fame career. He is the only pitcher with more than 2,000 career strikeouts as a Cub.

4 **Philadelphis Phillies Acquire Jim Bunning** – The Phillies sent Don Demeter to the Tigers for Bunning, winner of 110 games in the previous 7 seasons, but winner of only 12 in 1963. Bunning became the Phillies' ace, winning 74 games over the next 4 seasons, and becoming the first Twentieth Century pitcher to win more than 100 games in each league.

5 **Chicago White Sox Acquire Hoyt Wilhelm** –At the end of the 1962 season, Chicago got the 39-year-old Wilhelm (along with Dave Nicholson, Ron Hansen and Pete Ward) for shortstop Luis Aparicio and outfielder Al Smith. In the next 6 seasons, Wilhelm appeared in 361 games, winning 41 and saving 98, with a combined ERA of 1.92.

Maury Wills

The Man Who Brought Theft Back in Style

The National League's 1962 Most Valuable Player hit under .300 that year. (No, he wasn't a pitcher.) He walloped a mighty total of 6 home runs that year, and drove in all of 48 runs.

In addition to being an excellent shortstop (a 2-time Gold Glove winner), the Dodgers' Maury Wills did one thing exceptionally well: steal bases. He was so good at stealing bases that he won the Most Valuable Player award in 1962 while leading the league in that offensive category and no other. And with Wills' accomplishment, the 1960s witnessed the fall of another unbreakable record, this time at the expense of the game's greatest all-time hitter and base runner.

When Ty Cobb stole 96 bases in 1915, the stolen base was still a primary offensive weapon, right along with the bunt and sacrifice fly. Cobb's brand of baseball prided itself on an economy

---

Outstanding Feat

When Maury Wills stole 104 bases in 1962, he was caught stealing only 13 times. Ty Cobb, the player whose stolen base record Wills broke, was caught stealing 38 times when he stole 96 bases in 1915.

---

of runs, backed by pitching and defense. The popularity of that kind of baseball – both within the game and among fans – did not survive Babe Ruth and the more "lively" baseball of the 1920s and beyond.

Fast-forward to 1962. Cobb's stolen base record survived his passing in 1961. While excitement about the chase for Cobb's record never quite reached the fervor that hounded Roger Maris, Wills' assault on Cobb's record definitely engaged the country, and again extended baseball's impact beyond the everyday fan, much the same as the quest for Ruth's home run record had accomplished the year before.

Bats: Both **Throws:** Right
Height: 5' 11" **Weight:** 170 lb.

Born: October 2, 1932 in Washington, DC
Debut: June 6, 1959
Final Game: October 4, 1972

As the 1962 pennant race entered September, Wills had 73 stolen bases. He needed 23 more to catch Cobb, and had 27 games left to do it (19 games if he wanted to match Cobb in 154 games and avoid the expanded schedule controversy that haunted Maris). He stole 4 bases in one Friday night game against Pittsburgh, bringing his total to 82. In the next week he stole 9 more, giving him 91 after 148 games. Stolen base 95 came against the Cardinals in Game #154. Wills tied and passed Cobb's mark with 2 stolen bases in Game #156. He ended the season with 104 stolen bases.

Wills never bested that total. The closest he came was with 94 stolen bases in 1965. During his 14-season career, Wills averaged 49 steals per season, leading the league five different times.

Did You Know ...

Maury Wills was the major leagues' second African-American manager, skippering the Seattle Mariners for 82 games during the 1980 and 1981 seasons.

Top 5 Relief Pitchers of the 1960s

1 Hoyt Wilhelm – Riding his trademark knuckleball all the way to Cooperstown, Wilhelm was a dominating pitcher for 21 years. Throughout the 1960s, he won 75 games and saved 152 more, with an ERA of 2.19 for the decade.

2 Dick Radatz - During his rookie season with the Boston Red Sox in 1962, Radatz appeared in 62 games, going 9-6 with a 2.24 ERA, striking out 144 batters in 124 innings pitched, and leading the major leagues with 24 saves. His dominance continued over the next 2 seasons. In 1963, Radatz finished 58 of the 66 games he appeared in, going 15-6 with a 1.97 ERA and 25 saves. That year he struck out 162 batters in only 132 innings.

3 Ron Perranoski – Perranoski established himself as the Dodgers' closer in 1962, appearing in 70 games and finishing 39 of them, with 20 saves and a 2.85 ERA. In 1963, Perranoski had a career year, with a 16-3 record and 21 saves with a 1.67 earned run average. Over the next 4 years, Perranoski appeared in 256 games for the Dodgers, saving 54 with a 2.73 ERA.

4 Roy Face – Face's best season came in 1959, when he set the major league record for winning percentage (.947) on an 18-1 record. In 1960, Face went 10-8 for the world champion Pittsburgh Pirates, with 24 saves and a 2.90 ERA on a league-leading total of 68 appearances. He led the league again in saves in 1961 (17) and in 1962 (28), when he had the lowest ERA of his career (1.88).

5 Phil Regan – As a reliever for the Los Angeles Dodgers and Chicago Cubs from 1966 to 1969, Regan went 44-21 with a 2.60 ERA and 69 saves. His best year was 1966, when he went 14-1 for the Dodgers with a 1.62 ERA and a league-leading 21 saves. He also led the league with 25 saves in 1968, splitting a 12-5 season between the Dodgers and the Cubs.

Dick Radatz

The Monster of the Midway

During his short career, Dick Radatz more than any other pitcher redefined the role of reliever and ushered in the era of relief specialist that had such a profound impact on major league baseball in the second half of the Twentieth Century.

At 6-foot-5 and 235 pounds, Radatz was an imposing figure on the mound. He threw hard and with less than pinpoint accuracy, keeping hitters off balance and often swinging defensively at his heat. There was no finesse to his pitching style. He entered the game with one job: to blow the baseball past the hitter. For three years in the mid-1960s, no one did it better.

Radatz was signed by the Boston Red Sox out of Michigan State University in 1959. He made the big league club in 1962 and his impact was immediate. During his rookie season, the right hander appeared in 62 games and finished 53 of them. He went 9-6 with a 2.24 ERA. He struck out 144 batters in 124 innings pitched, and led the major leagues with 24 saves.

Outstanding Feat

During his first 3 seasons, Dick Radatz averaged 1.18 strikeouts per inning.

His dominance continued over the next 2 seasons. In 1963, Radatz finished 58 of the 66 games he appeared in, going 15-6 with a 1.97 ERA and 25 saves. That year he struck out 162 batters in only 132 innings. In 1964, Radatz led the majors with 29 saves, finishing 67 games in 79 appearances, and posting a 16-9 record with a 2.29 ERA. He struck out 181 batters in 157 innings pitched.

Radatz never achieved those kinds of numbers again. As his fastball began to fade, so did his performance, going 9-11 in 1965 with a 3.91 ERA. Though he still recorded 22 saves in 1965, he struck out fewer batters than innings pitched for the first time in his career. He was winless in 1966, going 0-5 with a 4.64 ERA and only 14 saves in a season split between Boston and Cleveland. He hung on through 1969, making stops with the Chicago Cubs, Detroit Tigers and Montreal Expos. In the last 3 years of his career, Radatz was a combined 3-6 with only 8 saves.

Bats: Right **Throws:** Right
Height: 6' 5" **Weight:** 235 lb.

Born: April 2, 1937 in Detroit, MI
Debut: April 10, 1962
Final Game: August 15, 1969

Without the fastball, Radatz couldn't be effective. But when he had it, nearly every batter was a strikeout waiting to happen.

Hank Aaron

Underappreciated Genius with a Bat

Was Hank Aaron so good that, despite his staggering career statistics and a boatload of offensive records, he might have been the most underrated slugger in baseball history?

Maybe ... Hank was that good. He wasn't as flashy as Mays and Clemente. Or as charismatic as Mantle or Musial. Or as powerful as Killebrew or even his own teammate, Eddie Mathews. Kids didn't fight over his baseball cards. He was simply the poster child for quiet, consistent excellence. He didn't scream for your attention. You knew he was there, collecting his hits and RBIs, but didn't really give him much thought. Then a couple decades went by, and Hank Aaron retired with more home runs (755), RBIs (2,297), extra-base hits (1,477) and total bases (6,856) than anyone else who ever played the game – including Babe Ruth.

... if only he had been respected by the fans as much as he was

> *Outstanding Feat*
>
> *Hank Aaron was the only player in major league history to hit 20 or more home runs for 20 consecutive years.*

by the pitchers who faced him.

Hank Aaron's performance in the 1960s was as outstanding and consistent as any period in his career. While the 1960s were probably Aaron's most productive period personally, the Braves' supporting cast was generally not equal to the caliber of the Braves teams of the late 1950s. After being runner-up to the Pirates in 1960, the Braves could finish no higher than 4th place from 1961 to 1968. Thus Aaron didn't really have the opportunity to shine in the national media spotlight of a tight pennant race.

From 1960 to 1969, Hank Aaron led the major leagues twice in runs scored and 3 times in RBIs. He hit over .300 in 8 different seasons during the decade, and scored at least 100 runs in 9 out of the 10 years. His only post-season appearance during the 1960s was in the first National League Championship Series in 1969. The fact that the New York Mets swept the Braves on the way to their "miraculous" championship overshadowed Aaron's performance in that Series. In 3 games, he hit .357 with 2 doubles, 3 home runs and 7 RBIs.

> **Bats:** Right **Throws:** Right
> **Height:** 6' 0" **Weight:** 180 lb.
>
> **Born:** February 5, 1934 in Mobile, AL
> **Debut:** April 13, 1954
> **Final Game:** October 3, 1976
> **Inducted into the**
> **Baseball Hall of Fame**: 1982

It was a fitting symbol for Aaron in the 1960s: outstanding performance, largely overlooked.

Sandy Koufax

Ace of Aces

No superlative can do justice to the performance of Sandy Koufax in his prime. In a decade dominated by overpowering pitchers, none was more dominating or overpowering than the Dodgers' hard-throwing southpaw.

With the 1960s version of Koufax, every start was probably going to be a victory, possibly going to be a shutout, and potentially going to be a no-hitter. (He pitched 4.) Most pitchers never experience even a single 20-win season. In his last 5 years (1962-1966) Koufax won 25 games or more 3 times; in the other two years, he was on track to win at least 25 games when injuries cut short both seasons – just as they would later abbreviate his career.

Outstanding Feat

Of his 4 no-hitters, the last one – on September 9, 1965 – was a perfect game. Koufax beat the Cubs 1-0 that night, striking out 14. He needed only 1:43 to complete his pitching gem.

A career-long Dodger (who never played in the minors), Koufax was mediocre at best in his first 6 seasons. A great arm and inconsistent control led to a 36-40 record, with season ERAs consistently above 3.00 and often higher than 4.00.

The change over the last 6 years of his career couldn't have been more dramatic. On the verge of retiring out of frustration, Koufax worked in the 1960 off-season to re-engineer his pitching mechanics. Something clicked, and his walks per 9 innings declined steadily from near 6.0 to as low as 1.7 in 1965. His numbers for hits and strikeouts per nine innings remained pretty much the same. The key for Koufax was control. Once he mastered it, there was no stopping him.

Bats: Right **Throws:** Left
Height: 6' 2" **Weight:** 210 lb.

Born: December 30, 1935 in Brooklyn, NY
Debut: June 24, 1955
Final Game: October 2, 1966
Inducted into the
Baseball Hall of Fame: 1972

His break-out year was 1961, when he won 18 games with his best ERA up to that point, a respectable 3.52. Koufax led the majors in strikeouts for the first time (269) and pitched 15 complete games. In 1962, he started fast, winning 14 games by the All-Star break. Yet injuries brought his season (and for all intents and purposes, the Dodgers' pennant hopes) to a halt as Koufax didn't win another game the rest of the year. Even with his shortened season, Koufax led the league with a 2.54 ERA. From this point until the season following his retirement, no one else would lead the National League in earned run average.

The Koufax era of dominance began in earnest in 1963. With the benefit of a complete and healthy season, Koufax racked up a 25-5 record with 306 strikeouts and a 1.88 ERA. He led the majors in all three of those pitching categories, as well as topping all major league pitchers with 11 shutouts. He won both the Cy Young and Most Valuable Player awards for 1963. And in the 1963 World Series against the Yankees, Koufax spearheaded the Dodgers' 4-game sweep with 2 victories, the latter a Series-clinching 2-1 victory.

In 1964, Koufax was leading the league in nearly every pitching category when he injured his pitching elbow while sliding into base. The injury ended his season with 6 weeks still remaining. He finished 19-5 (good for fourth in victories). Despite missing a month and a half, Koufax ended up fourth in strikeouts with 223, and led the majors in ERA (1.74) and shutouts (7).

The elbow Koufax damaged in 1964 continued to bother him for the next two years, but you wouldn't know that from his statistics. In 1965, he went 26-8, with a 2.04 ERA, a major league record 382 strikeouts in 335 innings, and 27 complete games – leading the majors in all of those categories. He was even better in 1966, going 27-9 with a 1.73 ERA, 317 strikeouts in 323 innings, with 27 complete games and 5 shutouts – again leading the major leagues in all of those categories. He was the unanimous Cy Young award winner both seasons.

Having Koufax available to pitch full seasons meant a National League pennant for the Dodgers in both 1965 and 1966. Koufax won two games as the Dodgers defeated the Minnesota Twins in the 1965 World Series. He lost in his only appearance in the 1966 World Series as the Baltimore Orioles swept the Dodgers.

That 6-0 loss to the Orioles (and to a 20-year-old future Hall of Famer named Jim Palmer) marked Koufax's last major league appearance. He retired in November of 1966 as a consequence of continued arthritic deterioration of his left elbow. He was only 30. In 1972, Koufax at age 36 became the youngest man elected to the Baseball Hall of Fame.

Did You Know ...

When Sandy Koufax was signed by the Dodgers and immediately placed on their major league roster, room was made for the hard-throwing rookie by dropping another pitcher: Tommy Lasorda.

Ernie Banks

A Cub with Clout

When you think of Ernie Banks, you think the engaging smile, the gentlemanly grace both on the field and off, the quick bat ... and all that power.

Banks was an offensive star for the Cubs starting in his rookie season of 1954, hitting .275 with 19 homes runs and 79 RBIs – respectable hitting numbers for any major league shortstop. But Banks was to redefine the power and run production standards for a shortstop, starting the next season when he hit .295 with 44 home runs and 117 RBIs. Banks continued his onslaught against National League pitching through the rest of the 1950s, hitting 40+ home runs each year from 1957 through 1960, and winning the league's Most Valuable Player award in both 1958 and 1959.

Outstanding Feat

In 1960, Ernie Banks became the first shortstop to lead his league in home runs and win a Gold Glove in the same season. In fact, Banks' 41 round-trippers were tops in the major leagues that year.

46

60 From The '60s

Throughout the 1960s, Banks was a consistent offensive threat despite the fact that he played for mostly sub-.500 Cub teams. During the decade, first as the Cubs' shortstop and later as the team's first baseman, Banks averaged 27 home runs and 95 RBIs per season. During the Cubs' ill-fated pennant chase of 1969, Banks closed out the decade with a fine year, batting .253 with 23 home runs and 106 RBIs.

Banks was a Cub for his entire career, 19 seasons during which he hit 512 home runs and drove in over 1600 runs. Banks finished his career as the leader in

Bats: Right **Throws:** Right
Height: 6' 1" **Weight:** 180 lb.

Born: January 31, 1931 in Dallas, TX
Debut: September 17, 1953
Final Game: September 26, 1971
Inducted into the
Baseball Hall of Fame: 1977

career home runs by a shortstop (277). His total still ranks third today (behind Cal Ripken and Alex Rodriguez, respectively). Banks was elected to the Baseball Hall of Fame in 1977.

Did You Know ...

Durability was a hallmark of Ernie Banks' career. In 12 of his 19 seasons, Banks played 150 or more games, leading the league in games played in 6 out of his first 7 seasons.

Whitey Ford

The Babe's Other Nemesis

The 1960s were not particularly kind to baseball's most legendary player. First Roger Maris assaulted Babe Ruth's supposedly "unbreakable" record for home runs in a season. The same year Maris hit 61 round-trippers, a Ruth pitching record, for consecutive scoreless innings pitched in the World Series, was being threatened by another Yankee.

Left-hander Whitey Ford, a Yankee starter for more than a decade, hit his peak in the early 1960s. From his rookie season in 1950 (9-1, 2.81 ERA) through 1960, Ford never won more than 19 games in a season. In 1961, Ford dominated American League hitters, going 25-4 with a 3.21 ERA.

That year Ford led the majors in winning percentage (.862) and innings pitched (283) to win the Cy Young award, which acknowledged the best pitcher in baseball. (NOTE: Individual league Cy Young awards didn't begin until 1967.) He followed

Outstanding Feat

Whitey Ford's career ERA (2.75) is the lowest of any post-World War II pitcher – including Sandy Koufax (2.76).

that excellent season with four more strong campaigns: 17-8 with a 2.90 ERA in 1962, 24-7 with a 2.74 ERA in 1963, 17-6 with a 2.13 ERA in 1964, and 16-13 with 3.24 ERA in 1965. Ford retired after the 1967 season with a .690 winning percentage, the highest of any Twentieth Century pitcher. Ford was elected to the Baseball Hall of Fame in 1974.

One of Ford's qualifications for entrance into the Hall was his sterling career record in the World Series. In 11 different Series he won 10 games with a 2.71 ERA over 146 innings. Babe Ruth's record for consecutive scoreless World Series innings pitched (29.2) was set in 1918 when Ruth was a member of the Boston Red Sox. Ford's streak started in 1960, when he shut out the Pirates twice. In the 1961 World Series against the Cincinnati Reds, Ford opened the Series with a 2-hit, 2-0 whitewash, his third consecutive World Series shutout. He now had 27 consecutive scoreless innings, 2.2 behind the Babe.

Bats: Left **Throws:** Left

Height: 5' 10" **Weight:** 181 lb.

Born: October 21, 1928 in New York, NY

Debut: July 1, 1950

Final Game: May 21, 1967

Inducted into the

Baseball Hall of Fame: 1974

Ruth's record lasted until Game 4 of the 1961 World Series. Ford pitched 5 more scoreless innings before he was forced to leave the game due to an ankle injury. Yankee right-hander Jim Coates finished the 7-0 shutout with 4 innings of scoreless relief, and Ford had the record at 32 consecutive scoreless innings – a record he still holds today.

Lou Brock

Sweet Speed

The most famous – and productive – trade in St. Louis Cardinals history was made on June 15, 1964. The Cardinals sent 2 former 20-game winners, Ernie Broglio and Bobby Shantz, along with outfielder Doug Clemens, to the Chicago Cubs for 3 players: Pitchers Jack Spring and Paul Toth, and an outfielder named Lou Brock.

For the Cubs, the trade worked out this way: Broglio went 4-7 for the rest of that year and 7-19 for the Cubs over 3 years. Shantz went 0-1 for the Cubs before being purchased by the Philadelphia Phillies in August. Clemens hit .279 with 12 RBIs in 54 games with the Cubs. (He hit .221 for Cubs the next year.) For the Cardinals, the trade worked out this way: Spring pitched in only 2 innings. Toth never made an appearance. Brock, however, led the Cardinals to the World Series, and followed up with a career that led to his eventual enshrinement in Cooperstown.

Lou Brock had a fabulous second half for the Cardinals in 1964. In 103 games, he hit .348 and scored 84 runs, with 9 triples, 12 home runs, 44 RBIs and 33 stolen bases. He was the offensive spark plug for a Cardinal team that won its first pennant since

Outstanding Feat

Lou Brock eventually broke Maury Wills' single-season record for stolen bases with 118 in 1974.

1946. In the World Series against the New York Yankees, Brock was instrumental in helping St. Louis take the championship, batting .300 with 5 RBIs and 9 hits in 7 games, including 2 doubles and a home run.

Brock's performance was no fluke. He led the league in stolen bases each year from 1966 to 1969. His best year offensively was during the Cardinals' pennant-winning season of 1967. Brock had career highs in hits (206), triples (12), home runs (21), RBIs (76) and batted .299. He led the majors with 113 runs scored.

In the 1967 World Series against the Boston Red Sox, Brock hit .414 with 12 hits and 3 stolen bases as the Cardinals took the Series 4 games to 3. In 1968, Brock capped another strong regular season – when he led the major leagues in doubles

Bats: Left **Throws:** Left
Weight: 170 lb.

Born: June 18, 1939 in El Dorado, AR
Debut: September 10, 1961
Final Game: September 30, 1979
Inducted into the
Baseball Hall of Fame: 1985

(46), triples (14), and stolen bases (62) – by elevating his performance again in the Fall Classic. Against the Detroit Tigers, Brock hit .464 with 13 hits, including 3 doubles, a triple and 2 home runs. Brock also drove in 5 runs and stole 7 bases.

Brock finished his career with the Cardinals, retiring in 1979 with 3,023 hits and, at the time, the career record for stolen bases with 938. He was the most prolific base stealer during the 1960s, with 430. Brock was elected to the Baseball Hall of Fame in 1985.

Harmon Killebrew

One Mistake and He'd Kill You

Few sluggers in the 1960s – or for that matter, any era – could match the raw power of Harmon Killebrew. What may have been most amazing about his slugging ability was how anyone who swung the bat as hard as Killebrew could be so productive so consistently and for so long.

Signed as a "bonus baby" in 1954, Killebrew played all but the last season of his 22-year career with the Senators/Twins organization. His first full season with the Senators was 1959, when he led the American League with 42 home runs. It was the first of 8 seasons in which Killebrew would hit 40 or more home runs, leading the league in homers 6 times.

Outstanding Feat

On July 18, 1962, Harmon Killebrew hit 2 grand slams in a game against the Cleveland Indians. (Another Twin, Bob Allison, also hit a grand slam in that game – in the same inning as Killebrew's first bases-loaded bomb.)

60 From The '60s

The Twins featured one of the most potent line-ups during the 1960s, anchored by Killebrew in the clean-up position. He drove in 100 or more runs in a season 9 times during his career. His highest RBI total came in 1969, with 140 to go with 49 home runs, both major league highs. He was voted Most Valuable Player that year, as he also led the league in walks (145) and on-base percentage (.427).

Killebrew retired after the 1975 season, hitting 573 home runs in his career, an average of 1 home run for every 14 at-bats. He was inducted into the Baseball Hall of Fame in 1984.

Bats: Right **Throws:** Right
Height: 5' 11" **Weight:** 213 lb.

Born: June 29, 1936 in Payette, ID
Debut: June 23, 1954
Final Game: September 26, 1975
Inducted into the
Baseball Hall of Fame: 1984

Did You Know ...

Some of Harmon Killebrew's strength with a bat may have been genetic in origin. His father had been a college fullback and professional wrestler, and his grandfather was reputed to have been the strongest man in the Union Army during the Civil War.

Al Kaline

The Gentleman Tiger

Al Kaline was the ultimate blue-collar ballplayer in the major leagues' ultimate blue-collar town. His 20-year career consisted of steady productivity punctuated with flashes of brilliance. He was a gentleman ballplayer whom everyone respected and no one – not even his opponents – could dislike.

A career-long Tiger, Kaline never played an inning of minor league ball, going right from high school to Detroit's outfield. He collected an American League batting championship before turning 21, hitting .340 in 1955.

During the 1960s, you could count on Kaline for 20+ home runs, 80+ RBIs and a batting average around .300 year in and year out. His best season during the 1960s came in 1963, when he batted .312 with 27 home runs and 101 RBIs. A superb outfielder, Kaline won 7 consecutive Gold Gloves from 1961 to 1967, and earned 10 overall in his career.

Outstanding Feat

At age 20, Al Kaline was baseball's youngest-ever batting champion, a distinction he still holds.

In his only World Series appearance in 1968, Kaline batted .379 as the Tigers bested the Cardinals 4-3. In seven games, Kaline had 11 hits, including 2 doubles and 2 home runs. He scored 6 runs and drove in 8.

Kaline retired in 1974 after collecting 3,007 hits during his 22-season career. He was elected to the Baseball Hall of Fame in 1980.

Bats: Right   **Throws:** Right
Height: 6' 2"   **Weight:** 180 lb.

Born: December 19, 1934 in Baltimore, MD
Debut: June 25, 1953
Final Game: October 2, 1974
Inducted into the
Baseball Hall of Fame: 1980

Did You Know ...

Al Kaline played in 18 All-Star games over a 20-year span (1955 to 1974).

Don Drysdale

Baseball's Best-Slugging Pitcher

There was no designated hitter in the 1960s, which was a break for Los Angeles Dodgers pitcher Don Drysdale. He was one of the best hitting pitchers in baseball history, as well as the Dodgers' best right hander through the 1960s.

A Dodger for his entire career, Drysdale blasted 29 home runs during his 14-season career, sixth on the all-time list among major league pitchers. Among pitchers, he ranked second among the all-time leaders in most home runs in a season (with 7 – which Drysdale did twice). He was also one of the few pitchers in major league history to win 20 games and bat .300 in the same season. In 1965, Drysdale hit .300 (with a career-high 19 RBIs) while going 23-12 on the mound, with 210 strikeouts, 7 shutouts and a 2.77 ERA.

Outstanding Feat

During his last full season in 1968, Don Drysdale broke Walter Johnson's major league record for consecutive scoreless innings with 56.2, amassed over a streak of 6 consecutive shutouts

---

Drysdale's best season pitching was 1962, when he won the Cy Young award for 25-9 record, the most victories among major league pitchers that season. Drysdale was dominant that year, leading the majors in games started (41), innings pitched (314) and strikeouts (232). In a four-year span from 1962 to 1967, Drysdale won 85 games and, with Sandy Koufax, formed the most devastating pitching duo in baseball.

Arm problems forced his retirement in 1969, with a career record of 209-166 with a 2.95 career ERA. He was elected to the Baseball Hall of Fame in 1984.

Bats: Right   **Throws:** Right
Height: 6' 6"   **Weight:** 216 lb.

Born: July 23, 1936 in Van Nuys, CA
Debut: April 17, 1956
Final Game: August 5, 1969
Inducted into the
Baseball Hall of Fame: 1984

Did You Know ...

Never afraid to back hitters off the plate, Don Drysdale finished his career with a total of 154 hit batsmen, the highest in National League history.

Mickey Mantle

The Mighty Mick

It is said that, when he started with the Yankees in the 1950s, Mickey Mantle possessed – among his many physical skills – tremendous speed on the base paths and in the outfield (hence one of his nicknames … the Commerce Comet).

By the 1960s, injuries had taken their toll on the Mick's legs. But he still had *bat* speed … enough to make him one of the most dangerous hitters in the American League for the first half of the decade. Not to take anything away from Roger Maris' tremendous achievements in 1960 and 1961, but it's unlikely that Maris would have seen the quality of pitches he received had Mantle not been hitting behind him.

Mantle led the American League with 40 home runs in 1960, the last year he would lead the league in that category. He swatted 54 home runs (with 128 RBIs) to finish second to Maris in 1961.

Outstanding Feat

Always an outstanding post-season hitter, Mickey Mantle shredded the Pittsburgh pitching staff during the 1960 World Series. He batted .400 in the 7-game series, collecting 10 hits (including 3 home runs) and drove in 11 runs.

Injuries limited his playing time and home run output to 30 in 1962 and 15 in 1963. However, his 30 home runs with 89 RBIs and a .321 batting average in 1962 (in only 123 games and 377 official at-bats) were good enough to earn Mantle his third Most Valuable Player award.

Mantle's power numbers rebounded in 1964 with 35 home runs (and 111 RBIs). He wouldn't hit that many home runs again in a season, retiring after the 1968 season. Yet during the 9 years he played during the 1960s, Mantle hit nearly half of his 536 career home runs.

Mantle was a lethal force for producing runs in the first half of the decade, especially in tandem with Maris, and was integral to the Yankees winning 5 consecutive American League pennants. This 16-time All-Star, and probably the best switch hitter in baseball history, was elected to the Baseball Hall of Fame in 1974.

Bats: Both   **Throws:** Right
Height: 5' 11"   **Weight:** 198 lb.

Born: October 20, 1931 in Spavinaw, OK
Debut: April 17, 1951
Final Game: September 28, 1968
**Inducted into the
Baseball Hall of Fame**: 1974

Carl Yastrzemski

Three Batting Titles and a Triple Crown

It must be nice to be able to replace one Hall of Fame outfielder with another one. The Yankees did when Joe DiMaggio relinquished centerfield to Mickey Mantle. And the Red Sox followed suit a decade later, replacing the great Ted Williams, who retired at the end of the 1960 season, with a pure hitter named Carl Yastrzemski.

Yaz was the prototype for the complete ballplayer, hitting for power and average and playing left field superbly throughout his 23 major league seasons, all with the Red Sox. He was signed as a

Outstanding Feat

In the last 12 games of the 1967 pennant race, Carl Yastrzemski came through for the Red Sox when they needed him most. He hit 5 home runs, scored 14 runs and drove in 16.

free agent in 1958 and debuted in left field for the Red Sox in 1961. He hit .266 as a rookie, driving in 80 runs. The next year he raised his batting average to .296, with 19 home runs and 94 RBIs. His offensive numbers would only get better.

In 1963, Yastrzemski hit .321 to win his first American League batting title. That year, he also led the league in hits (183), doubles (40) and bases on balls (95). He continued hitting well over the next three years, leading the league in doubles in 1965 and 1966. He failed to repeat as doubles leader in 1967, but he compensated in other ways.

1967 was a miracle season for Yastrzemski and the Red Sox. The team won the American League pennant by one game in a three-team race that came down to the last day of the season. Yaz almost single-handedly carried the Red Sox to the pennant. In the last two "must win" games against the Minnesota Twins, Yastrzemski went 7 for 8 with 6 RBIs.

Bats: Left **Throws:** Right
Height: 5' 11" **Weight:** 182 lb.

Born: August 22, 1939 in Southampton, NY
Debut: April 11, 1961
Final Game: October 2, 1983
Inducted into
the Baseball Hall of Fame: 1989

When the regular season had ended, Yastrzemski was at the top of the league in nearly every offensive category: hits (189), runs (112), home runs (44, tied with Minnesota's Harmon Killebrew), RBIs (121), total bases (360), slugging percentage (.622) and batting average (.326). His Triple Crown leadership in home runs, RBIs and batting average earned Yaz the league's Most Valuable Player award. During the 1967 World Series, which the St. Louis Cardinals won in 7 games, Yastrzemski continued his offensive onslaught, batting .400 with 3 home runs.

In 1968, Yastrzemski won his third batting title with a .301 average – the league's only .300 hitter that year and the lowest average ever for a batting champion. He closed out the 1960s with another superb year in 1969, hitting 40 home runs and driving in 111 runs, though he hit only .255. He won the Gold Glove for his consistent excellence in left field 5 times during the 1960s, and 6 times in all during his career.

Yastrzemski retired with 3,419 major league hits, #7 all time. The last of the Triple Crown winners was voted into the Baseball Hall of Fame in 1989.

Did You Know ...

Carl Yastrzemski's 23 seasons with the Boston Red Sox tie the major league record for seasons with a single franchise. Yaz shares the record with Brooks Robinson of the Baltimore Orioles.

Top 5 Hitting Performances of the 1960s

1 **Roger Maris hits 61 home runs** – Maris turned the baseball world upside down in 1961 when he broke the game's most sacred record and, some believed, its most unbreakable: Babe Ruth's single-season home run mark of 60 set in 1927.

2 **Frank Robinson wins the Triple Crown**. – Traded to Baltimore following the 1965 season, he was considered to be on the downside of his career. Robbie answered that criticism with a vengeance, as he led the American League in the Triple Crown categories (.316, 49 home runs, 122 RBIs) as well as in runs scored (122), total bases (367), on-base percentage (.410) and slugging percentage (.637).

3 **Roberto Clemente takes 4 batting titles**. Roberto Clemente was the major leagues' leading hitter for the 1960s, averaging a combined .328 for the decade. He was batting champion 4 times during the decade: in 1961 (.351), in 1964 (.339), in 1965 (.329) and in 1967 (.357).

4 **Frank Howard strings together 6 consecutive home run games**. – During the 1968 season, Howard led the majors in home runs (44), slugging percentage (.552), and total bases (330). During one 6-game streak, he blasted 10 home runs in 20 at-bats.

5 **Tony Oliva's rookie season**. – During his 1964 debut season, Oliva led the American League in 5 different offensive categories: hits (217), runs (109), doubles (43), total bases (374) and batting average (.323).

Camilo Pascual

Señor Curveball

If, as most observers at the time believed, the best curveball in the 1960s belonged to Sandy Koufax, the second best – and a close second at that – was delivered by a right-handed, Cuban-born pitcher named Camilo Pascual.

He had a curveball that dropped as if it were falling off the edge of an invisible table. And he used it to win more games than he should have for teams that supported him less than they should have.

Pascual was signed by the Washington Senator as an amateur free agent in 1952. His rookie year in the big leagues was 1954, when he went 4-7 as a reliever for the Senators. Only 4 of his 48 appearances that year were starts. (Those were the days when most young pitchers had to earn their way into the starting rotation … via the bullpen.)

From 1955 to 1958, Pascual started in the Senators' regular rotation. Pitching for one of the worst teams in the American

---

Outstanding Feat

In both 1962 and 1963, Camilo Pascual was the only American League pitcher to reach the 200 strikeouts mark.

League, Pascual's combined record for those 4 years was 24-59. But as his strikeout-to-walk ratio gradually improved, his extraordinary stuff took over and his record improved to 17-10 in 1959 with a 2.64 ERA. He led the majors in both complete games and shutouts that year, and followed with a 12-8 record in 1960, the team's last year in Washington.

For the next 4 years, pitching for the same franchise in a new location, Pascual was clearly the ace of the Minnesota Twins' staff. He won 15 games in 1961, leading the American League in strikeouts with 221 and leading the major leagues with 8 shutouts. He would repeat as the American League strikeout leader again in each of the next two years, winning 20 games in 1962 and 21 in 1963. His 18 complete games in

Bats: Right   **Throws:** Right
Height: 5' 11"   **Weight:** 185 lb.

Born: January 20, 1934 in Havana, Cuba
Debut: April 15, 1954
Final Game: May 5, 1971

both of those years were tops in the league.

Pascual went 15-12 for the Twins in 1965, with career highs in both starts (36) and innings pitched (267). At 31, Pascual was already on the down slope of his career, winning only 44 games over the next 5 years. He retired in 1971 with an 18-year record of 174-170 and a 3.63 ERA. For the four years when Pascual was one of the American League's right-handers, his combined record was 71-48 with 842 strikeouts and a 3.18 ERA.

Dean Chance

Chance Favors the Hard Throwing

Between 1963 and 1966, only one pitcher *not* named Koufax won the Cy Young award. That was Wilmer Dean Chance, the Los Angeles Angels ace who hurled 11 shutouts in 1964.

Signed by Baltimore in 1959, the Los Angeles Angels plucked Dean Chance from the Orioles' organization in the 1960 expansion draft. In his rookie season of 1962, Chance emerged as the team's best starter, finishing with a 14-10 record and 2.96 ERA as the Angels surprised the league by finishing third in only their second season of existence. The next year the Angels came back to earth, finishing ninth, and Chance's record slipped to 13-18 despite pitching well enough to post a 3.19 ERA.

Chance was the American League's most dominant pitcher in 1964, his Cy Young season. His 20-9 record tied him with Chicago's Gary Peters for most victories. Chance led the league in inning pitched (278) and complete games (15), of which 11 were shutouts. He also recorded the majors' best ERA at 1.65. His 207

Outstanding Feat

Among the 11 shutouts Dean Chance pitched during the 1964 season, 6 of them were 1-0 victories.

strikeouts were third highest in the league.

The 1965 season was another strong one for Chance, 15-10 with a 3.15 ERA. The next year, he lowered his ERA to 3.08, but his record slipped to 12-17. That winter, Chance was traded to the Minnesota Twins for Pete Cimino, Jimmie Hall and Don Mincher.

Chance won 20 games for the Twins in 1967 with a 2.73 ERA. He led the American League in games started (39), complete games (18) and innings pitched (283). He was third in the American League in strikeouts with 220. The only dark point for Chance in an otherwise stellar season came on the last day.

The Twins were tied with the Red Sox going into the last regular season game at Fenway Park. It was a marquee pitching matching, pitting Chance (20-13) for the Twins, and Jim Lonborg (21-7) for the Red Sox. The Twins scored a run in both the first and third innings, while Chance shut out the Red Sox over the first five frames.

Bats: Right   **Throws:** Right

Height: 6' 3"   **Weight:** 200 lb.

Born: June 1, 1941 in Plain Township, OH

Debut: September 11, 1961

Final Game: August 9, 1971

Then the Red Sox chased Chance out of the game, scoring 5 times in the sixth inning. Lonborg coasted the rest of the way, winning a league-leading twenty-second game and the Cy Young award.

In 1968, Chance went 16-16 for the Twins with an excellent 2.53 ERA. He achieved personal highs for innings pitched (292) and strikeouts (234). A series of injuries kept Chance from ever again performing at that level. Over the next 3 years, pitching for 4 different teams, Chance's combined record was only 18-19.

Did You Know ...

When Dean Chance threw 11 shutouts in 1964, the Angels' team total was 28, the most shutouts by a single major league team since the 1909 Chicago Cubs (32).

Top 5 Third Basemen of the 1960s

1 **Brooks Robinson** - Brooks Robinson had a Gold Glove for every year in the 1960s – 16 in all during his career. Robinson was also a consistent batting threat in the heart of the Baltimore Orioles' batting order. His best offensive year was 1964, when he won the American League Most Valuable Player award by batting .317 with 28 home runs and a league-leading 118 RBIs.

2 **Ron Santo** – Santo's offensive production, combined with sterling defense, made him one of the best all-around third basemen of all time. From 1964 through 1969, Santo averaged 24 home runs and 104 RBIs per season for the Chicago Cubs. He hit .297 over that period, and led the league in walks for 4 of those years. He was also the best defensive third baseman in the National League, winning 5 consecutive Gold Gloves between 1964 and 1968.

3 **Dick Allen** – Allen won Rookie of the Year honors in 1964, leading the major leagues in runs (125) and triples (13) while batting .318 with 201 hits, 29 home runs and 91 RBIs. Allen was a consistent threat as Philadelphia's All-Star third baseman during the 1960s, averaging 29 home runs and 90 RBIs per season from 1964 to 1969, and batting a combined .300 over that period.

4 **Ken Boyer** – Boyer won 5 Gold Gloves as the Cardinals' third baseman, and averaged 23 home runs with 91 RBIs and a .293 batting average during his Cardinal career. His all-around play and championship-caliber leadership earned Boyer 1964's National League Most Valuable Player award.

5 **Tony Perez** - Tony Perez had a long and productive career that began in the 1960s and continued until 1986. From 1967 through 1969, he was a mainstay already in the Cincinnati offense, hitting .289 over that period as he averaged 27 home runs and 105 RBIs per season.

Brooks Robinson

Where Line Drives Went To Die

Throughout the decade of the 1960s, Brooks Robinson was simply the best third baseman in baseball.

He was a vacuum cleaner at third base. He got to every ball he should have fielded, and handled most balls that no one should have been able to get to.

He was not blessed with speed, but his incredible reflexes and a strong, accurate throwing arm allowed him to turn hits into outs with amazing consistency. No wonder there were so many winning pitchers on the Orioles' staff throughout the 1960s.

Robinson had a Gold Glove for every year in the 1960s – 16 in all during his career. Those who had the privilege of seeing

> *Outstanding Feat*
>
> *Brooks Robinson won 16 consecutive Gold Gloves for his third base play. The only other player to match that streak was pitcher Jim Kaat.*

Robinson at third never really had the opportunity to take his excellence for granted. He simply too often did too many things no third baseman should be able to do to allow complacency on the part of the fans. He was that good.

When Robinson retired, he held practically every career fielding record for a third baseman, including most career putouts (2,697), most career assists (6,205), most career double plays (618), and the highest fielding average (.971).

Robinson was also a consistent batting threat in the heart of the Orioles' batting order. His best offensive year was 1964, when he won the American League Most Valuable Player award by batting .317 with 28 home runs and a league-leading 118 RBIs. His hitting alone wouldn't have put him in the Hall of Fame. But 2 decades of consistently productive hitting, along with his spectacular fielding, did.

Bats: Right **Throws:** Right
Height: 6' 1" **Weight:** 190 lb.

Born: May 18, 1937 in Little Rock, AK
Debut: September 17, 1955
Final Game: August 13, 1977
Inducted into the
Baseball Hall of Fame: 1983

Did You Know ...

Brooks Robinson appeared in every All-Star game during the 1960s, and was chosen as MVP for the 1966 game.

Bobby Richardson

Yankee Anchor, World Series Dynamo

As the New York Yankees were winning 5 consecutive American League pennants and appearing in 5 World Series during the first half of the 1960s, one thing all those seasons had in common was the consistent performance of the team's second baseman, particularly in the Fall Classic.

Bobby Richardson was a Yankee for his entire career, starting in 1953 when he was signed as an amateur free agent. Bobby broke in with the Yankees in 1955 and was the part-time second baseman starting in 1957. By 1959, when Richardson hit .301, he was firmly entrenched in the Yankee infield.

Outstanding Feat

Bobby Richardson was involved in a career-high 136 double plays in 1961, the twelfth highest total for a second baseman in major league history.

72

60 From The '60s

From 1961 through 1966, the durable Richardson never had fewer than 600 official at-bats in a season. He led the American League in hits in 1962 with 209. That year he had a career-high .302 batting average, and finished second in the MVP balloting to teammate Mickey Mantle. He was the league's Gold Glove second baseman from 1961 to 1965. He retired after the 1966 season.

Richardson's most valuable work for the Yankees came when it counted most … in October. His limited appearances in the 1957 and 1958 Series produced no hits. But when the Yankees returned to the Series in 1960, their now full-time second baseman proved to be the Yankees' most productive hitter. In that 7-game Series pitted against the Pittsburgh Pirates, Bobby Richardson drove in 12 runs on 11 hits, including 2 doubles, 2 triples and a home run. For the Series, he batted .367 with a .667 slugging percentage, a performance that earned him the Series MVP despite the fact that the Pirates won the championship.

Bats: Right **Throws:** Right
Height: 5' 9" **Weight:** 170 lb.

Born: August 19, 1935 in Sumter, SC
Debut: August 5, 1955
Final Game: October 2, 1966

The Yankees won the 1961 World Series in five games against the Cincinnati Reds, and Richardson again was a hitting star, batting .391. In the 1964 World Series against the St. Louis Cardinals, Richardson pounded out 13 hits in the 7-game series, batting .406. In 36 World Series games spanning 7 different series, Richardson hit .305, nearly 40 points higher than his career batting average.

In the 1962 Series against the San Francisco Giants, Richardson struggled at the plate, hitting only .148 for the Series, but he was pivotal in the decisive seventh game. The game was played at Candlestick Park in San Francisco. The Yankees' pitcher, right-hander Ralph Terry, had won 23 games during the regular season. He was also the pitcher who gave up the walk-off homer to Bill Mazeroski in the 1960 heartbreak loss to the Pirates.

Terry was brilliant against the Giants, pitching a two-hitter and taking a 1-0 lead into the bottom of the ninth. Pinch-hitter Matty Alou led off with a bunt single. Terry responded by striking out Felipe Alou and Chuck Hiller. Then Willie Mays, who had hit 49 home runs and driven in 141 RBIs during the regular season,

doubled to right. Roger Maris speared the ball on the run and fired a strike to Richardson at the cut-off, holding the speedy Alou at third.

The next batter, a young Willie McCovey, had hit 20 home runs with 54 RBIs during the regular season. Walk him to set a force out at any base, and Terry would have had to face first baseman Orlando Cepeda, who had driven in 144 runs during the regular season. The Yankees elected to pitch to McCovey.

McCovey, the future Hall of Famer, worked Terry to a 1-1 count. The next pitch was a fastball. McCovey turned on it and sent a screaming drive to right field, except …

The 5-foot-9 Richardson literally rose to the occasion, leaping and snagging the line drive to end the inning and the Series. With his bat or his glove, Bobby Richardson was money in the bank for the Yankees at World Series time.

Top 5 Sluggers of the 1960s

1 **Hank Aaron** – Aaron was huge in just about every offensive category during the 1960s. He led the National League in home runs 3 times in totaling 375 homers for the decade. He drove in more runs (1,107) than any other hitter in the 1960s, leading the league 3 times in RBIs, and posted the highest slugging average for the decade (.565).

2 **Willie Mays** – Mays also led the National League in home runs three times during the 1960s, hitting 350 dingers during the decade. He averaged 100 RBIs per season and hit for a slugging average of .559 during the 1960s.

3 **Frank Robinson** – Robinson's 316 home runs were fourth best for the decade, and his 1,011 RBIs during the 1960s were third best among major leaguers. His .560 slugging average was second only to Aaron. He led his league in home runs, RBIs and batting only once, but accomplishing that all in 1966 earned him the Triple Crown. Neither Aaron nor Mays ever did that.

4 **Harmon Killebrew** – The Minnesota Twins first baseman blasted more home runs (393) in the 1960s than any other player. Harmon Killebrew led the American League in home runs 5 times during the decade, and ranked second in RBIs for the decade (1,013) and fifth in slugging percentage (.546).

5 **Willie McCovey** – The 1960s were the first decade to produce 5 hitters with 300 or more homes runs, and number 5 on that list, with 300, was McCovey, though he was a part-time player for the first 4 years of the decade. In the 6 seasons that he played full-time, he led the National League in home runs 3 times.

Ron Santo

All Cub, No Flub

R on Santo was one of the best defensive third basemen of the 1960s (close but no Brooks Robinson – no one else was). He was maybe one of the best all-around third basemen of all-time. He was that good.

As a high school player out of Seattle, Santo was recruited by all 16 major league teams, signing with the Cubs in 1959. He was called up to join the Cubs' roster midway in 1960, batting .251 with 9 home runs and 44 RBIs in 95 games.

In 1961, Santo's first full season, he hit .284 with 23 home runs and 83 RBIs. By 1963 Santo was an All-Star, that year hitting .297 with 25 home runs and 99 RBIs. He was an All-Star for 5 of the next 6 seasons, and a fixture at third for the Cubs for the next decade. From 1964 through 1969, Santo averaged 24 home runs and 104 RBIs per season. He hit .297 over that period, and led the league in walks for 4 of those years. He was the poster child for offensive consistency.

Outstanding Feat

Though he suffered from diabetes throughout his career, Ron Santo proved to be incredibly durable, averaging 160 games per year from 1962 through 1969.

76

Santo was a power hitter with strike-zone discipline. In 4 different seasons, he led the National League in bases on balls. Twice he led the league in on-base percentage. And though he suffered from diabetes throughout his career, Santo proved to be incredibly durable, averaging 160 games per year from 1962 through 1969.

Santo was also the best defensive third baseman in the National League. He won 5 consecutive Gold Gloves between 1964 and 1968. For his career, Santo holds or shares the National League record for years leading the league in chances (9), assists (7) and double plays (6).

Bats: Right **Throws:** Right
Height: 6' 0" **Weight:** 190 lb.

Born: February 25, 1940 in Seattle, Washington
Debut: June 26, 1960
Final Game: September 29, 1974

Santo's 337 career home runs put him fifth all-time among third basemen. He was elected to the Baseball Hall of Fame in 2011.

Did You Know ...

Ron Santo is one of the few major league players to play for more than one team, but spend his entire career in only one city (Chicago, closing out his career with the White Sox for one season).

Warren Spahn

The Ageless Arm

The winningest left-handed pitcher in major league history, Warren Spahn could just as easily appear in a book of great players from the 1940s and 1950s. And while the 1960s were, for him, the least productive of his three chronological decades as a ballplayer, Spahn had some of his best years in the early 1960s, continuing his run of pitching excellence well past age 40.

Spahn's professional baseball career began prior to World War II, as he was signed as an amateur free agent by the Boston Braves in 1940. He debuted for the Braves in 1942, appearing in only 4 games before returning to the minors. A tour in the U.S. Army kept Spahn out of the major leagues until his discharge in 1946. In 1947 he went 21-10, the first of 13 20-victory seasons in his career. From 1947 through 1959, Spahn won 259 games with a 2.94 ERA. In those 13 seasons, he led the National League in victories 6 times, in ERA twice, and in strikeouts 4 times.

Outstanding Feat

During his career, Warren Spahn pitched 63 shutouts, the most by any lefthander.

Spahn turned 39 at the beginning of the 1960 season, but his excellence on the mound continued. From 1960 to 1963, he won 83 games, leading the league twice in victories and topping the National League all 4 years in complete games. His 3.02 ERA was the league's best in 1961. In both 1960 and 1961, Spahn finished second in the Cy Young award voting. (His only Cy Young title came in 1957.)

Spahn also pitched his only no-hitters during the 1960s, shutting down the Phillies in September of 1960 and blanking the Giants the following April. In 1961, Spahn became the first National League lefthander to post 300 career victories.

He ended his 21-season career with the San Francisco Giants in 1965 after starting the season with the New York Mets. The rest of his career was with the Braves. His 363 career victories (plus 4 World Series wins) put him at the top among all southpaws. He was elected to the Baseball Hall of Fame in 1973.

Bats: Left **Throws:** Left
Height: 6' 0" **Weight:** 175 lb.

Born: April 23, 1921 in Buffalo, NY
Debut: April 19, 1942
Final Game: October 1, 1965
Inducted into the
Baseball Hall of Fame: 1973

Did You Know ...

A terrific hitter for a pitcher, Warren Spahn smacked 35 career home runs, tied (with Bob Lemon) for second-best all-time among pitchers (Wes Ferrell had 37).

Orlando Cepeda

Bullish on Slugging

If you want to know how good a ballplayer Orlando Cepeda was in his prime, consider this: for more than 6 years, he kept a future Hall of Famer with 521 career home runs out of the starting line-up.

That player was the great Willie McCovey, one of the most feared hitters in National League history, and deservedly so. But in the early 1960s, McCovey wasn't good enough to displace Cepeda from first base in the Giants' starting line-up.

Though remembered as a slugger himself, Cepeda (nicknamed "The Baby Bull") was actually a well-rounded ballplayer. He was signed by the Giants in 1955, and was San Francisco's starting first baseman by the beginning of the 1958 season. He was the National League's Rookie of the Year that season, hitting .312 with 25 home runs, 96 RBIs and 15 stolen bases. He also led the league with 38 doubles. In his second season he was even better, hitting .317 with 27 home runs, 105 RBIs and 23 stolen bases.

Outstanding Feat

Orlando Cepeda's major-league-leading mark of 142 RBIs in 1961 was one better than Willie Mays' career best, but only ranks second all-time for the Giants franchise. Hall-of-Famer Mel Ott tops the list with 151 RBIs in 1929.

In 1961, Cepeda led the league in both home runs (46) and RBIs (142) while hitting .311. He finished second in the MVP voting to Cincinnati's Frank Robinson. From 1960 through 1964, Cepeda batted a combined .307, averaging 34 home runs and 109 RBIs per season.

During weight training following the 1964 season, Cepeda injured a knee, and tried playing through the injury without telling team management. Knee surgery sidelined him for most of the 1965 season, and in 1966 the Giants traded Cepeda to the St. Louis Cardinals. In 1967, Cepeda captured the National League's Most Valuable Award as the offensive leader of the pennant-winning Cardinals. He hit .325 with 25 home runs and a league-leading 111 RBIs. His power numbers slipped to 16 home runs and 73 RBIs as the Cardinals repeated as National League champions in 1968.

In the spring of 1969, Cepeda was traded to the Atlanta Braves for catcher-first baseman Joe Torre. His 22 home runs and 88 RBIs played an integral

Bats: Right **Throws:** Right

Height: 6' 2" **Weight:** 210 lb.

Born: September 17, 1937 in Ponce, P.R.

Debut: April 15, 1958

Final Game: September 19, 1974

Inducted into the

Baseball Hall of Fame: 1999

role in the Braves' divisional championship. The following year, Cepeda had his last strong season, hitting .305 for the Braves with 34 home runs and 111 RBIs. He retired in 1974 with 379 home runs and a career batting average of .297. He was elected to the Baseball Hall of Fame in 1999.

Luis Aparicio

Great Hands, Amazing Feet.

In the 6 years before Maury Wills "resurrected" the stolen base as an offensive weapon, another shortstop was using the stolen base – and two of the surest hands in baseball – in launching a career that led straight to Cooperstown.

Speed and defense made Luis Aparicio the American League's premier shortstop from the mid-1950s to the mid-1960s. His impact on the league was almost immediate. A native of Venezuela, Aparicio was signed by the White Sox as an amateur free agent in 1954 and was Chicago's starting shortstop in his rookie season two years later. The year, 1956, marked the first of 9 consecutive years when Aparicio led the American League in steals (with a career high of 57 in 1964). He was selected as Rookie of the Year for the 1956 season.

As the team's lead-off hitter, Aparicio was the spark plug for the White Sox offense until he was traded to the Baltimore Orioles

Outstanding Feat

The 342 bases Luis Aparicio stole during the 1960s ranks him first among American League base stealers during that decade.

82

prior to the 1963 season (in a deal that included Ron Hansen and future Hall of Fame reliever Hoyt Wilhelm). He played for the Orioles for 5 years, leading the league twice in stolen bases and winning 2 of his 9 Gold Gloves during his tenure in Baltimore. Aparicio was traded back to the White Sox before the 1968 season, closing out the 1960s with the Pale Hose. Aparicio retired after the 1973 season, his third year with the Boston Red Sox.

An 11-time All-Star, Aparicio collected 2,677 hits on a career batting average of .262, with a total of 506 stolen bases. Aparicio played more games at shortstop than any other player in major league history (2,581) and retired with more assists (8,016) than any other shortstop in history. (Today he still ranks #2 in this category behind Ozzie Smith.) He was elected to the Baseball Hall of Fame in 1984.

Bats: Right   **Throws:** Right
Height: 5' 9"   **Weight:** 160 lb.

Born: April 29, 1934 in Maracaibo, Venezuela
Debut: April 17, 1956
Final Game: September 28, 1973
Inducted into the
Baseball Hall of Fame: 1984

Did You Know ...

Luis Aparicio was the first native of Venezuela to be elected to the Baseball Hall of Fame.

Juan Marichal

Baseball's Greatest Second-Best Pitcher

During the 1960s, he won more games (191) than Sandy Koufax (137), Bob Gibson (163) and Denny McLain (114) – but never won a Cy Young award.

During the 1960s, he struck out more batters (1,840) than Sam McDowell (1,663) and Camilo Pascual (1,391) – but never led his league in that category.

During the 1960s, he posted a combined ERA of 2.57 -- lower than the decade ERAs for Bob Gibson (2.74), Dean Chance (2.77) and Whitey Ford (2.83) -- but won his league's ERA crown only once in a 16-year career.

In any other decade, Juan Marichal might have been the game's most dominant pitcher. But in the pitching-rich 1960s, he was "simply" one of a group of truly great, Hall of Fame pitchers – and quite probably the decade's most underrated hurler.

> *Outstanding Feat*
>
> *In 1963, Juan Marichal pitched a 16-inning shutout to beat the Milwaukee Braves and Warren Spahn 1-0.*

84

Marichal was a delight to watch, in terms of both style and effectiveness. One of the last of the "high kick" hurlers, his delivery encompassed a panorama of release points, from straight over the top to sidearm and all point in-between. He utilized a vast repertoire of pitches, with variations on his fastball, curveball and change-up that constantly kept hitters off-guard. He could throw hard. He pitched with control.

A native of the Dominican Republic, Marichal was signed by the New York Giants in 1957. He made his debut with the San Francisco Giants in 1960, and found a place in the starting rotation almost immediately.

In the Giants' pennant-winning season of 1962, Marichal won 18 games, but that was only third best on the team (behind Jack Sanford's 24-7 and Billy O'Dell's 19-14). He went 25-8 (including a no-hitter) in 1963, the same year Sandy Koufax won the Cy Young Award

Bats: Right   **Throws:** Right
Height: 6' 0"   **Weight:** 185 lb.

Born: October 20, 1937 in Laguna Verde, D.R.
Debut: July 19, 1960
Final Game: April 16, 1975
Inducted into the
Baseball Hall of Fame: 1983

with a 25-5 season. He followed that in 1964 with a 21-8 record, leading the majors with 22 complete games and posting a 2.48 ERA. However, he lost out on the Cy Young Award to the Angels' Dean Chance, who had the most productive season of his career at 20-9 with 11 shutouts and a 1.65 ERA.

In 1965, Marichal won 22 games with a major-league best 10 shutouts and a 2.13 ERA. That same season Koufax won 26 games with a 2.04 ERA and his second Cy Young Award. Marichal followed in 1966 with a spectacular season, posting a 25-6 record with a 2.23 ERA. Again that year, Koufax topped him, going 27-9 with league-leading 1.73 ERA.

In 1968, Marichal had his best season, finishing the year 26-9 with a 2.43 ERA. He led the league in victories, innings pitched (326) and complete games (30). But that was the year Bob Gibson swept both the Most Valuable Player and Cy Young awards with a 22-9 record with a 1.12 ERA in leading the St. Louis Cardinals to their second consecutive pennant. Marichal closed out the 1960s with a 21-11 record in 1969, posting a major-league best 2.10 ERA while leading the league in shutouts with 8.

Marichal finished his career with 243 wins and a 2.89 ERA. A 9-time All-Star (and MVP of the 1965 All-Star Game), Marichal was elected to the Baseball Hall of Fame in 1983.

Did You Know ...

When he retired in 1975, Juan Marichal's 52 shutouts put him in ninth place among right-hand pitchers for career whitewashes.

Juan-derful Debut

Starting a Hall of Fame Career with a One-Hit Masterpiece

While not significant in the 1960 pennant race, the July 19 game between Philadelphia and San Francisco was significant in baseball history ... as the dazzling debut of future Hall of Famer Juan Marichal.

Marichal started the game by striking out Phillies shortstop Ruben Amaro. He then retired Tony Taylor and Johnny Callison for a perfect first inning. He retired the Phillies in order again in the second inning, and the third. Marichal's pitching stayed perfect through the sixth inning ... 18 Phillies batters, 18 Phillies outs.

That perfect game evaporated in the seventh inning. After striking out Amaro, Marichal allowed his first baserunner of the game as Taylor reached first on an error by Giants shortstop Eddie Bressoud. A wild pitch that advanced Taylor to second base was followed by a walk to first baseman Pancho Herrera. The runners were stranded as Joe Morgan flied out to Willie Mays in center field.

Phillies catcher Clay Dalrymple
His eighth-inning pinch single was the lone hit ...

Meanwhile, the Giants had already given Marichal all the runs he would need. In the second inning, an RBI single by third baseman Jim Davenport scored Orlando Cepeda. Willie Kirkland's single in the fifth inning drove in Willie Mays with the game's second and final run.

Marichal retired the first 2 batters in the eighth inning before allowing a single by pinch-hitter Clay Dalrymple. Tony Gonzalez fouled out to end the inning with Dalrymple still at first. Then Marichal retired the Phillies in order in the ninth.

That's how to start a baseball career: Retire the first 17 batters you face, and finish the game with a 1-hit shutout, 12 strikeouts and only 1 walk. Phillies starter John Buzhardt deserved better in the loss, allowing only 2 runs over 7 innings. But when you're pitching against the man who would win more games in the 1960s than any other major league pitcher, you better bring Hall of Fame stuff.

... allowed by Juan Marichal in his major league debut.

Top 5 Left Fielders of the 1960s

1 **Lou Brock** –Brock was the spark plug for a St. Louis Cardinals team that won it all in 1964. Playing in 103 games after being acquired from the Cubs, Brock hit .348 and scored 84 runs, with 9 triples, 12 home runs, 44 RBIs and 33 stolen bases. Brock finished his career with the Cardinals, collecting 3,023 hits and, at the time, the career record for stolen bases with 938.

2 **Carl Yastrzemski** – For 23 seasons, Yastrzemski owned left field in Fenway Park. During the 1960s (he joined the Red Sox in 1961), Yaz won 3 batting titles, a Triple Crown and MVP in 1967, and 5 Gold Gloves.

3 **Rocky Colavito** - Rocky Colavito played outfield for 6 different teams during the 1960s. He hit 45 home runs with 140 RBIs for Detroit in 1961, and led the American League with 108 RBIs as a member of the Cleveland Indians in 1965. From 1960 through 1966, he averaged 32 home runs and 101 RBIs per season.

4 **Billy Williams** – Billy Williams started the 1960s as the National League Rookie of the Year and ended the decade on the verge of setting the NL record for consecutive games played (which he did in September of 1970 with 1,117). In between he batted a combined .292 for the decade, averaging 27 home runs and 94 RBIs per year. (He would win a batting title in 1972.)

5 **Willie Horton** – The Detroit Tigers left fielder was the team's most dangerous power hitter through the second half of the 1960s, averaging 27 home runs and 89 RBIs per year. Willie Horton's best overall year was 1968, when he hit .285 with 36 home runs. He hit 325 home runs over an 18-year career.

Roberto Clemente

He Made Excellence Look Easy

Roberto Clemente was so good at every baseball skill, and so naturally fluid at everything he did, that sometimes you had to wonder whether he was truly human. His untimely death in a 1972 plane crash on his way to help survivors of a Nicaraguan earthquake regrettably proved that he was mortal. But so often it didn't seem that way on the baseball field.

Signed by the Brooklyn Dodgers in 1952, Clemente was acquired by the Pittsburgh Pirates in the 1954 amateur draft. He spent the rest of his career as a member of the Pittsburgh organization. It was during the 1960s that Clemente emerged as one of the game's premier players.

Outstanding Feat

Roberto Clemente had one of the most powerful and accurate throwing arms of any outfielder. He once threw out a third-base runner at home plate – off a single to right!

90

Beginning in 1960, he hit .300 or better every season for the rest of his career except for 1968 – the "Year of the Pitcher" in baseball – when Clemente's batting average "slipped" to .291.

Clemente won his first batting title in 1961 with a .351 average. He repeated as National League batting champion in 1964 (.339), 1965 (.329) and 1967 (.357), when he also led the majors with 209 hits. Never considered a power hitter, Clemente's highest single-season home run total came in 1966 when he belted 29 home runs and drove in 119 runs. He was voted National League Most Valuable Player that year. For his career, Clemente averaged 87 RBIs per season.

Hitting was only part of Clemente's arsenal of baseball skills. He had great speed and was an aggressive base runner, though he was never really concerned

Bats: Right **Throws:** Right
Height: 5' 11" **Weight:** 175 lb.

Born: August 18, 1934 in Carolina, P.R.
Debut: April 17, 1955
Final Game: October 3, 1972
Inducted into the
Baseball Hall of Fame: 1973

with stealing bases. Clemente's forte was turning line drives into doubles and stretching doubles into triples. He led the majors in triples once, with 12 in 1969 (when he hit .345). His career total of 166 triples was the most by any right-handed hitter in the post-World War II era.

Clemente was the game's finest right fielder during the 1960s. His arm was strong and his throws extremely accurate. His 266 career assists as an outfielder remain unmatched in the modern era. He was the National League's only Gold Glove right fielder throughout the 1960s, and won 12 Gold Glove awards over his career.

In post-season play, Clemente actually *elevated* his game. In the 1960 World Series against the New York Yankees, Clemente batted .310 with 9 hits and 3 RBIs in the 7-game series. He hit safely in all 7 games, a feat he repeated in the 1971 World Series against the Baltimore Orioles.

Clemente collected career hit number 3,000 in the last game of 1972, his last season. He was inducted posthumously into the Baseball Hall of Fame in 1973.

Did You Know ...

In 1965, Roberto Clemente played the full season and led the league with a .329 batting average ... despite have contracted malaria that year.

Almost a Dodger . . .

How Roberto Clemente Became a Pirate.

While his entire major league career was spent playing for the Pittsburgh Pirates, Roberto Clemente was not originally signed by the Bucs.

Clemente was originally signed as a free agent in 1954 by the Brooklyn Dodgers, reportedly for a $5,000 signing bonus. At that time, any team signing a player for a bonus and salary of more than $4,000 had the choice of keeping him on the major league roster for two years or risk losing him in the off-season draft. Rather than let the 19-year-old Clemente (still a raw talent) languish on the Dodgers' bench, the club assigned him to its top minor league affiliate in Montreal.

In his first three months for the Montreal Royals, Clemente was strictly platooned and in fact played rarely. Part of the reason that Clemente played so sparingly was that the Montreal roster was loaded with talented future major leaguers. In addition, the Dodgers no doubt preferred to hide their new talent rather than showcase him just to be snatched away in the winter draft.

But a talent like Clemente's is hard to hide, and he was playing every day by the end of the season, his only year in the minors.

93

It's hard to imagine Hall of Famer Roberto Clemente in Dodger blue ... but it nearly happened.

The Pittsburgh Pirates, who had the first selection in the draft, used it to take Clemente. He made the big league club that year, hitting .255 as a rookie, and spent the next 17 years in a Pirate uniform, collecting 3,000 hits, 4 batting titles and 12 Gold Gloves along the way.

What if the Dodgers had protected Clemente and kept him on their major league roster? Imagine a Dodger team throughout the 1960s with Clemente in right field instead of Ron Fairly or Lou Johnson. Both were good, solid ballplayers who made valuable contributions to the Dodgers' success in the 1960s. But there was only one Clemente.

As good as they were, imagine how many more games Sandy Koufax and Don Drysdale might have won with Clemente spraying hits all over Chavez Ravine, and with his Gold Glove-caliber fielding behind them?

Top 5 Glove Men of the 1960s

1 **Bill Mazeroski** – Bill Mazeroski was the gold standard for Gold Glove players. He won 8 Gold Gloves and holds more defensive records than any other player in major league history, including being the only second baseman ever to record more than 1,700 double plays.

2 **Brooks Robinson** – Brooks Robinson was the premier third baseman during the 1960s. He had a Gold Glove for every year in the 1960s – 16 in all during his career. When Robinson retired, he held practically every career fielding record for a third baseman, including most career putouts (2,697), most career assists (6,205), most career double plays (618), and the highest fielding average (.971).

3 **Jim Kaat** –Kaat pitched in the majors for 25 years and was one of baseball's best-hitting pitchers throughout his career. As a fielder, Kaat had no peers among pitchers, and few major leaguers at any position fielded as well as he did. He won 16 consecutive Gold Gloves (matched only by Brooks Robinson). He also happened to win 283 games (#30 all time).

4 **Vic Power** – This first baseman was a 7-time Gold Glove winner. He led all American League first basemen in assists 6 years in a row. Power also tied a major league record with 2 unassisted double plays in a single game.

5 **Roberto Clemente** – The Pittsburgh Pirates' Hall of Fame right fielder could do it all in the field. Clemente won a Gold Glove every year from 1961 to 1972 – 12 in all. His arm was strong and his throws extremely accurate. His 266 career assists as an outfielder remain unmatched in the modern era.

Billy Williams

Such a Swing

The Chicago Cubs of the 1960s were something of an enigma: all that talent – especially in the heart of the line-up, and so little to show for it. (Of course, the same thing might also be said about the Cubs of the '20s, '30s, '40s, and '50s.)

How, with the likes of Ernie Banks and Ron Santo, did the Cubs struggle so hard to reach .500, much less contend? And add a Billy Williams to that equation, and the Cubs of the 1960s become all that much more puzzling.

Out of that trio of offensive superstars, Billy Williams might just have been the best hitter during the 1960s.

Williams was consistent, not spectacular. His swing was so compact, so smooth and sweet, that it's somewhat surprising that Billy Williams won only a single batting title during his 18-year career. He never led the league in home runs or RBIs, and led only once in runs and hits (both coming in 1970). But between 1961 and 1973, William never had fewer than 20 home runs or 84

Outstanding Feat

In 1970, Billy Williams set a new National League record for consecutive games played with 1,117. His record was broken in 1983 by Steve Garvey.

RBIs. All told, during those 13 seasons, he averaged 28 home runs with 98 RBIs, batting a combined .298. Five times during that period, he batted over .300.

Williams was Rookie of the Year in 1961 and an All-Star 6 times. He was a Cub for all but the last two seasons of his career, when he was a designated hitter for the Oakland A's (and made his only post-season appearance in the 1975 American League Championship Series, going hitless in 7 at-bats). He finished his career with more than 400 home runs and over 1400 RBIs.

He was elected to the Baseball Hall of Fame in 1987.

Bats: Left **Throws:** Right
Height: 6' 1" **Weight:** 175 lb.

Born: June 15, 1938 in Whistler, AL
Debut: August 6, 1959
Final Game: October 2, 1976
**Inducted into the
Baseball Hall of Fame**: 1987

Did You Know ...

While in the Chicago Cubs' minor league system, Billy Williams was personally tutored by Hall of Famer and 3-time .400 hitter Rogers Hornsby. Apparently, Williams was a good student, though his personal best batting average was "only" .333 in 1972.

Jim Bunning

Hall of Fame Senator Who Never Played for Washington

If you visit the Baseball Hall of Fame, you'll find six members who have been both pitchers and Senators. That group includes Walter Johnson, Clark Griffith, Early Wynn, Lefty Gomez and Stan Coveleski, all of whom played for Washington before the Senators moved to the Twin Cities in 1961.

The other pitcher, Jim Bunning, never pitched for Washington, though he did work there as a United States Senator from Kentucky. He earned his way to a place in Cooperstown by being a productive workhorse for 17 years. He was the first pitcher to win more than 100 games in each major league and the first to pitch a no-hitter in both leagues.

The Detroit Tigers signed Bunning out of Xavier University as a free agent. After 5 years in the Tigers' minor league system and 2 years appearing with Detroit part-time, Bunning broke into the

Outstanding Feat

On Father's Day in 1964, Jim Bunning pitched a perfect game against the New York Mets. It was his second career no-hitter, the first coming on July 7, 1958 against the Boston Red Sox.

starting rotation in 1957, going 20-8 and tying for the American League lead in victories (with Chicago's Billy Pierce) while leading the league in innings pitched with 267. His 2.69 ERA was third best in the league, and his 182 strikeouts were second by 2 to league-leader Early Wynn.

From 1960 to 1963, Bunning was the Tigers' premier starter, winning 59 games with a 3.36 ERA. The Tigers' workhorse averaged 256 innings and 192 strikeouts during those 4 years, but had winning records in only 2 of those seasons. In December 1963, the Tigers traded Bunning and catcher Gus Triandos to the Philadelphia Phillies for outfielder Don Demeter and pitcher Jack Hamilton. It was one of the best trades the Phillies ever made.

Bunning won 19 games in each of the next 3 years for the Phillies. In his 4-year

Bats: Right **Throws:** Right
Height: 6' 3" **Weight:** 195 lb.

Born: October 23, 1931 in Southgate, KY
Debut: July 20, 1955
Final Game: September 3, 1971
Inducted into the
Baseball Hall of Fame: 1996

tour with Philadelphia, Bunning won 74 games with a combined ERA of only 2.48. He averaged nearly 300 innings pitched and 250 strikeouts for those 4 seasons, leading the National League in strikeouts in 1967 with 253.

After stops in Pittsburgh and Los Angeles, Bunning returned to Philadelphia to close out his career. He retired in 1971 after 17 seasons that produced 224 career wins and a 3.24 ERA. During the 1960s, no one pitched more innings than Bunning (2,590) and only Juan Marichal (191) and Bob Gibson (163) recorded more victories than Bunning (150). A 9-time All-Star, Bunning was elected to the Baseball Hall of Fame in 1996, 2 years before he was elected to the U.S. Senate.

Did You Know ...

Jim Bunning pitched in 8 All-Star games (3 as the starter), but never in a post-season contest.

Top 5 First Basemen of the 1960s

1 **Harmon Killebrew** – Eight times in his career, Killebrew hit 40 or more home runs in a season, leading the league in home runs for 6 of those seasons. He drove in 100 or more runs in a season 9 times during his career. Killebrew retired following the 1975 season, hitting 573 home runs in his career.

2 **Willie McCovey** – The National League's Rookie of the Year in 1959, Willie McCovey led the National League with 44 home runs while driving in 102 runs in 1963. He led the league again in home runs and RBIs in both 1968 (36 and 105) and in 1969 (45 and 126). He was named National League Most Valuable Player for 1969.

3 **Orlando Cepeda** – In 1961, Cepeda led the league in both home runs (46) and RBIs (142) while hitting .311. From 1960 through 1964, Cepeda batted a combined .307, averaging 34 home runs and 109 RBIs per season. After struggling with knee injuries, Cepeda came back in 1967 as a member of the Cardinals to win the National League MVP by hitting .325 with 25 home runs and a league-leading 111 RBIs.

4 **Bill White** - White played first base for the St. Louis Cardinals and Philadelphia Phillies during the 1960s. He hit .286 over 13 seasons and collected 7 Gold Gloves, batting over .300 3 times and driving in more than 100 runs 4 times.

5 **Boog Powell** – Powell's .606 slugging percentage led the American League in 1964, and he helped the Orioles win the American League pennant in 1966 by hitting .287 with 34 home runs and 109 RBIs. He was outstanding in the Orioles' pennant-winning 1969 season with 37 home runs and 121 RBIs while hitting a career-high .304.

Frank Howard

Sometimes Size Counts

The 1968 season was the much ballyhooed "Year of the Pitcher" in both major leagues. That year the American League produced only a single .300 hitter (Carl Yastrzemski) and 5 pitchers with earned-run averages under 2.00, with 17 more sporting ERAs under 3.00. That year there were sharp declines in nearly every offensive category, as American League pitchers displayed unprecedented dominance over every hitter ... except one.

Huge Frank Howard, the towering outfielder and first baseman for the Washington Senators, had his own monster year in 1968, seemingly immune from the pitching excellence that stymied the rest of the league. That year, Howard batted .274 (.001 above his career average) with 106 RBIs (second in the league to Ken Harrelson's 109). Howard led the majors in home runs (44), slugging percentage (.552), and total bases (330).

At 6-foot-7 and 255 pounds, the right-handed-hitting Howard was always a threat to send the ball over the fence. Howard was

Outstanding Feat

In May of 1968, over a period of 6 games, Frank Howard hit 10 home runs in 20 at-bats, with at least one home run in each game.

signed by the Los Angeles Dodgers in 1958. After a couple brief stays with the big league club, Howard made the Dodgers' roster for good in 1960, hitting 27 home runs with 77 RBIs and being named National League Rookie of the Year. After injuries diminished his playing time and offensive numbers in 1961, Howard roared back in 1962 to hit .296 with 31 home runs and 119 RBIs.

Before the 1965 season, Howard was traded to the Washington Senators in a 6-player deal that sent left-handed pitcher Claude Osteen to the Dodgers. In his first two years with the Senators, Howard was productive but not outstanding. In 1967, his 36 home runs were double what he hit the previous year. Then came the 1968 season, when Howard

Bats: Right **Throws:** Right	
Height: 6' 7" **Weight:** 255 lb.	
Born: August 8, 1936 in Columbus, OH	
Debut: September 10, 1958	
Final Game: September 30, 1973	

emerged as the most feared power hitter in the league.

He was even better in 1969. He hit .296 with 111 RBIs and a career-best 48 home runs – 1 behind league leader Harmon Killebrew. He was spectacular again in 1970, leading the league in home runs (44), RBIs (126), and bases on balls (132).

Howard played 3 more years, but his power numbers declined each year. He closed out his 16-season career in 1973 with Detroit. He finished with 382 career home runs.

Bert Campaneris

Speed at Every Position

The Kansas City (and later, Oakland) Athletics had few bright spots during the 1960s. Six times during that decade, the A's lost at least 90 games, and three times lost more than 100. Prior to the introduction of divisional play in 1969, the Athletic' best finish was sixth in 1968, the first time in the 1960s that the A's finished above .500.

The only real bright spot for the franchise during the 1960s was the acquisition and development of a stable of young, talented players who would jell at the end of the 1960s and spur the Oakland Athletics' championship years in the early 1970s. One of the first of those foundation players was a fleet Cuban native named Dagoberto Campaneris.

Outstanding Feat

When Bert Campaneris led the American League with 51 stolen bases in 1965, he ended Luis Aparicio's 9-year reign as AL base-stealing champ (1956-1964).

60 From The '60s

"Bert" Campaneris came up with the A's as their shortstop in 1964, hitting a home run in his first at-bat and 2 homers in his first game. As an indication of things to come, that performance was misleading, as Campaneris' primary offensive weapon was speed, not power. Starting in 1965, Campaneris led the league in stolen bases in each of his first 4 seasons and in 6 out of his first 8 years with the A's. He led the league in triples in 1965 (12) and in hits in 1968 (177). During the 1960s, he batted a combined .264 with 292 stolen bases.

Campaneris was the A's shortstop and lead-off hitter for a dozen years. However, he was talented enough to play every position

Bats: Right **Throws:** Right
Height: 5' 10" **Weight:** 160 lb.

Born: March 9, 1942 in Pueblo Nuevo, Cuba
Debut: July 23, 1964
Final Game: October 1, 1983

and, on September 8, 1965, Campaneris did just that. In a night game against the California Angels, he played every position, giving up one run in the inning he pitched in a 5-3 loss (Campaneris did not figure in the decision).

A 5-time All-Star, Campaneris is still the Athletics' career leader in games (1,795), at-bats (7,180) and hits (1,882).

Did You Know ...

When Bert Campaneris played every position on September 8, 1965, his only error occurred in right field. He was error-free in 6 chances at other positions and, ironically, had no fielding chances during the inning he played his everyday position, shortstop.

Roger Craig

No Good Pitch Goes Unpunished

In a just universe, Roger Craig would be remembered and respected today as a fine pitcher versatile enough to start or relieve with equal effectiveness.

But Craig didn't pitch in that universe. He pitched in the National League at the turn of the 1960s. And if he's remembered at all, it's as the losingest pitcher for the one of the worst teams in major league history.

Craig was signed by the Brooklyn Dodgers in 1950. He won 19 games for 3 Dodger minor league teams in 1954 and was 10-2 for Montreal, Brooklyn's top minor league affiliate, in 1955 before being called up to the big leagues, where Craig was 5-3 with a 2.78 ERA for the Dodgers. Over the next 4 years, Craig was 31-26 as a spot starter and long reliever for the Dodgers. His earned run average for that period was 3.45, with 6 shutouts and one save.

Roger Craig continued to be a valuable hurler for the Dodgers as the 1960s began, filling in as needed by starting or relieving and

Outstanding Feat

Roger Craig was the winning pitcher in the fourth game of the 1964 World Series. Pitching for the St. Louis Cardinals against the New York Yankees, Craig worked 4.2 innings of scoreless relief, striking out 8, to earn the 4-3 decision.

generally pitching well. He was 8-3 in 1960 with a 3.27 ERA. In 1961, his last year with the Dodgers, Craig's record slipped to 5-6 with a 6.15 ERA. Based on that performance, the Dodgers left him unprotected, and he was selected by the New York Mets in the expansion draft.

The year 1962 was greeted with great excitement and anticipation in New York, where the National League hadn't played in more than 4 years. Roger Craig, a 49-38 starter-reliever for the Dodgers, was the Mets' ace in their inaugural season. He led the team in victories (10), innings pitched (233), hits (261), strikeouts (118, tied with Al Jackson) and complete games (13, tied with Jay Hook). He also led the team, and the league, in losses with 24. His 4.52 earned run average was a half-run lower than the team's. Little did Craig that this would be his *best* season with the Mets.

In 1963, Craig lowered his ERA to 3.78, but his victory total was cut in half as he went 5-22 for the Mets. His reward for pitching better,

Bats: Right **Throws:** Right
Height: 6' 4" **Weight:** 191 lb.

Born: February 17, 1930 in Durham, NC
Debut: July 17, 1955
Final Game: July 10, 1966

and having less to show for it, was to be traded to the St. Louis Cardinals for the 1964 season. He spent 1 season each with St. Louis, the Cincinnati Reds, and the Philadelphia Phillies, going a combined 10-14 with 9 saves over those 3 years (3.56 ERA). He retired after being released by the Phillies in 1966.

Dick Groat

No Shortage of Leadership

In the late 1950s and early 1960s, Dick Groat may have been the best all-around shortstop in baseball. Though he didn't have the speed to steal bases on a level with Luis Aparicio and Maury Wills, or the power to match the home run output of an Ernie Banks (before he moved to first base), Groat was a consistent .300 hitter for most of his career and an excellent shortstop, teaming with Pittsburgh Pirates second baseman Bill Mazeroski to form one of baseball's most prolific double play combinations.

Groat broke in with the Pirates in 1952, hitting .284 in 95 games. He spent the next 2 years out of organized baseball, first as a member of the NBA's Fort Wayne Pistons and then in the armed services. After completing his army service, Groat rejoined the Pirates as their starting shortstop, hitting .267 in his first full season. His hitting improved over the next three years, and his batting average topped .300 in both 1957 and 1958.

Outstanding Feat

On May 13, 1960, on the way to winning the National League batting title, Dick Groat went 6 for 6 (with 3 doubles) against the Milwaukee Braves.

The Pirates team that won the National League pennant in 1960 featured several star performances, but Groat was clearly the Bucs' day-to-day leader. As the National League batting champion with a .325 average, Groat also led the league in singles (154), finished third in hits (186), and was sixth in on-base percentage (.371). He was voted league Most Valuable Player for 1960, beating some formidable competition in Willie Mays (.319, 103 RBIs), Hank Aaron (40 home runs, a league-best 126 RBIs), and Ernie Banks (a league-leading 41 home runs and 117 RBIs). Besides his batting title, the most impressive "statistic" in Groat's favor was the Pirates' pennant – their first since 1927.

Following the 1962 season, Groat was traded to the Cardinals. He played well in

Bats: Right **Throws:** Right

Weight: 180 lb.

Born: November 4, 1930 in Wilkinsburg, PA

Debut: June 19, 1952

Final Game: October 1, 1967

1963, bouncing back from so-so offensive numbers the previous 2 years to hit .319 with 201 hits (his career best and second in the league to Vada Pinson's 204), 43 doubles (tops in the majors), 11 triples (third in the league) and a career-high 73 RBIs. He finished second to Sandy Koufax in the voting for the Most Valuable Player award.

Groat's numbers dropped only slightly in 1964, as he was an integral part of the Cardinals' pennant run. He hit .292 with 186 hits, 35 doubles and 70 RBIs. Before he retired in 1967, Groat also made stops in Philadelphia and San Francisco. An 8-time All-Star, Groat finished with a career batting average of .286.

Did You Know ...

As an All-American basketball player in the early 1950s, Groat set the NCAA individual record for points scored in one season with 851.

Top 5 Center Fielders of the 1960s

1 **Willie Mays** – From 1961 through 1965, Mays belted 226 home runs, more than a third of his 660 career total. His most productive season was 1965, when he led the majors in home runs (52), total bases (360), slugging average (.645) and on-base percentage (.399). He also won 8 Gold Gloves during the 1960s.

2 **Mickey Mantle** – For the first half of the 1960s, Mantle was a monster with a bat, leading the American League with 40 home runs in 1960, and swatting 54 home runs (with 128 RBIs) to finish second to Roger Maris in 1961. His 30 home runs with 89 RBIs and a .321 batting average in 1962 (in only 123 games and 377 official at-bats) were good enough to earn Mantle his third Most Valuable Player award.

3 **Curt Flood** – While better known today as the player who challenged baseball's reserve clause and opened the door to unrestricted free agency, Curt Flood's bat, glove and speed made him one of the premier center fielders during the 1960s. He played for the Cardinals throughout the 1960s, hitting .300 or better 6 times and winning a Gold Glove 7 times.

4 **Vada Pinson** – Pinson was a flawless center fielder who led the major leagues in doubles his first 2 seasons, and hit a career-high .343 to help the Reds win the National League pennant in 1961. Pinson drove in 100 or more runs in each of the next two years, leading the majors in hits (204) and triples (14) in 1963 while batting .313. For the 1960s, Pinson hit a combined .292.

5 **Jim Wynn** – As Houston's center fielder, Wynn led the team in home runs for 6 straight seasons (1965 to 1970). His best season was 1967, when he finished second in the league in home runs (37) and fourth in RBIs (107), both career highs. He hit more than 30 home runs in a season 2 more times, and remains third all-time in home runs (223) and RBIs (719) among Astros hitters.

111

Willie McCovey

Stretch for the Fences

Willie McCovey was synonymous with awesome power. The San Francisco Giants outfielder and first baseman was a power hitter who consistently made contact, and consistently inspired better pitches for the Giants batting in front of him.

McCovey was signed by the New York Giants in 1955, and made it to the big league club in 1959. In his debut, "Stretch" went 4 for 4 against future Hall of Famer Robin Roberts. Though he played only 52 games in his rookie year of 1959, his 13 homes runs, 38 RBIs and .354 batting average won him the Rookie of the Year award.

The Giants had an All-Star in Orlando Cepeda at first base, McCovey's natural position. So he platooned in the outfield, occasionally spelling Cepeda at first, and driving in only about 50 runs a year. In the Giants' pennant-winning season of 1962, McCovey hit .293 with 20 home runs and 54 RBIs in only 229 at-bats. His vicious line drive snared by the New York Yankees'

Outstanding Feat

Willie McCovey hit 2 home runs in a single All-Star Game (1969), one of only 4 players ever to do so.

second baseman Bobby Richardson to end the 1962 World Series was a fitting symbol for the frustration that typified McCovey's career up to that point: so much talent, and yet so little to show for it.

All that ended in 1963, as McCovey, playing his first full season with the Giants, led the National League with 44 home runs while driving in 102 runs. Injuries cut down his playing time and power numbers in 1964, but a healthy McCovey bounced back in 1965 with 39 home runs and 92 RBIs.

When Cepeda was traded to the St. Louis Cardinals in May of 1966, McCovey took over first base full-time for the Giants and was a power-hitting fixture there for the next 9 years. He closed out the 1960s as one of the most – if not *the* most – dangerous power hitter in all of baseball. He led the league in home runs and RBIs in both 1968 (36 and 105) and 1969 (45 and 126), when he finished 5th in the league in hitting with a .320 average. In 1969, he also led the major leagues in on-base

Bats: Left **Throws:** Left
Height: 6' 4" **Weight:** 210 lb.

Born: January 10, 1938 in Mobile, Alabama
Debut: July 30, 1959
Final Game: July 6, 1980
Inducted into the Baseball Hall of Fame: 1986

percentage (.453) and slugging percentage (.656). He was named National League Most Valuable Player for 1969.

In all, McCovey hit 300 home runs during the 1960s. His 22 big league seasons, with the Giants, the San Diego Padres and the Oakland Athletics, produced 521 home runs and over 1500 RBIs. A 6-time All-Star, he was elected to the Baseball Hall of Fame in 1986.

Did You Know ...

Willie McCovey finished his career with 18 grand slam home runs, second at the time only to Lou Gehrig's 23. (Today McCovey is tied for fourth in career grand slams.)

Top 5 Strikeout Pitchers of the 1960s

1 **Sandy Koufax** – Koufax averaged 9.51 strikeouts per 9 innings pitched during the 1960s, the highest average among all major league starting pitchers during that decade. He led the National League in strikeouts 4 times, and struck out more than 300 batters in a season 3 times.

2 **Bob Gibson** – With a total of 2,071, Bob Gibson recorded more strikeouts during the 1960s than any other pitcher. He averaged 7.62 strikeouts per 9 innings, and struck out 200 or more batters in a season 7 times. He was also the decade's best strikeout pitcher in the World Series, fanning 92 batters in 81 innings, including a record 17 in the first game of the 1968 World Series.

3 **Sam McDowell** – "Sudden" Sam led the American League in strikeouts 4 times during the 1960s (as well as in 1970), and topped 300 strikeouts in a season twice. Altogether, McDowell struck out 1,663 batters for the Cleveland Indians in the 1960s, though he pitched for only 6 full seasons during that decade.

4 **Jim Maloney** – The Cincinnati Reds right-hander struck out 1,585 batters during the 1960s, averaging 7.92 strikeouts per 9 innings. From 1963 through 1966, Maloney averaged 234 strikeouts per season while winning 78 games for the Reds.

5 **Bob Veale** – This 6-6 southpaw won 100 games for the Pittsburgh Pirates during the 1960s, including 18 victories in 1964, the year Veale led the National League in strikeouts with 250. He struck out 1,428 batters during the 1960s, an average of 7.98 strikeouts per 9 innings (third best among all pitchers).

Sam McDowell

Suddenly, You're Out!

His fastball was on top of the plate before you could get the bat off your shoulder. The break in his curve was nothing less than wicked. And his imposing stature on the mound made his heat, and occasional wildness, all the most intimidating.

"Sudden" Sam McDowell threw as hard as any pitcher of his time. And he struck out more American League batters (1,663) than anyone else in the 1960s.

McDowell was signed by Cleveland in 1959. He saw limited service with the Indians from 1961 to 1963, winning a total of 6 games in the major in those three years. His breakout year was 1964. After an 8-0 start at Portland, the Tribe's top minor league affiliate, McDowell was brought up to the major league club , where he went 11-6 with 177 strikeouts in 173 innings and registered a 2.70 ERA.

McDowell was dominating in his second full season with the Indians. He went 17-11 with a fifth-place Cleveland team.

Outstanding Feat

In 1966, Sam McDowell pitched back-to-back 1-hitters.

116

McDowell led the league in strikeouts with 325, still the American League record for a left-hander. Always better known for his "stuff" than his control, McDowell led the league in wild pitches (17) and walks (132) as well. He also posted the league's best ERA at 2.18.

Throughout the rest of the 1960s, despite consistently high strikeout totals and very respectable ERAs, McDowell was basically a .500 pitcher for the Indians. He led the league in strikeouts in 1966 (225), 1968 (283), and 1969 (279), finishing second with 236 to Jim Lonborg in 1967. In 1968 he posted a career-low ERA of 1.81 that was second best in the American League – to the 1.60 posted by teammate Luis Tiant. Despite these numbers, McDowell was only 55-51 for the years 1966 to 1969.

Although Mc Dowell's only 20-victory season came in 1970, his best performance may have come a year earlier. Pitching for a woeful Cleveland club that lost 99 games during the 1969 season (1 more than the expansion Seattle Pilots), McDowell

Bats: Left **Throws:** Left

Height: 6' 5" **Weight:** 218 lb.

Born: September 21, 1942 in Pittsburgh, PA
Debut: September 15, 1961
Final Game: June 24, 1975

was Cleveland's one bright spot that season. He went 18-14 with a 2.94 ERA and pitched 18 complete games.

A 6-time All-Star, McDowell finished his 15-year career with 141 victories and 2,453 strikeouts.

Ken Boyer

Cards' Big Deal at Third

Quietly and steadily, Ken Boyer was the leader of the St. Louis Cardinals through the first half of the 1960s. When the Cards were at their best, so was Boyer, winning the National League Most Valuable Player award in 1964, when the Cardinals won the World Series in 7 games over the New York Yankees (whose third baseman was Clete Boyer, Ken's younger brother).

When the Cardinals signed Boyer as an amateur free agent in 1949, they weren't quite sure what they had – except they knew they had a superb athlete. While he was groomed as a pitcher due to his strong right arm, Boyer hit over .300 in the minors, and finally found a home at third base. After a stint in the U.S. Army, Boyer joined the Cards to stay in 1955 and was their starting third baseman for the next decade.

Boyer was the soul of consistency, both in the field and at the plate. He won 5 Gold Gloves as the Cardinals' third baseman, and averaged 23 home runs with 91 RBIs and a .293 batting average. Boyer's best season was the Cardinals' championship season of

Outstanding Feat

In 1959, Ken Boyer had a 29-game hitting streak for the Cardinals, 4 shy of the team's record (held by Rogers Hornsby).

118

1964. He led the majors with 119 RBI that year. He batted .295 with 24 home runs and scored 100 runs. His all-around play and championship-caliber leadership earned Boyer the Most Valuable Player award in 1964.

He would never have a season like that again. Back problems in 1965 caused his batting average to slip to .260 and his power numbers dropped to 13 home runs and 75 RBIs. It was his last year with the Cardinals. St. Louis traded Boyer to the New York Mets for pitcher Al Jackson. For the next 4 years, as Boyer bounced from the Mets to the White Sox to the Dodgers, he never really recaptured the magic of his prime in St. Louis.

Bats: Right **Throws:** Right
Height: 6' 2" **Weight:** 200 lb.

Born: May 20, 1931 in Liberty, Missouri
Debut: April 12, 1955
Final Game: August 9, 1969

Did You Know ...

Ken Boyer was one of 3 Boyer brothers to play in the major leagues. Older brother Cloyd won 20 games in 5 major league seasons, 15 of those victories coming as a member of the Cardinals. Younger brother Cletis was the New York Yankees' third baseman from 1959 to 1966.

Vada Pinson

Playing in the Shadows

When people recall the Cincinnati superstars of the 1960s, names like Frank Robinson, Pete Rose, Tony Perez (and even Johnny Bench by the decade's end) come easily to mind. The Reds' "lost" superstar during that period was Vada Pinson, the sleek center fielder who consistently hit well in the heart of Cincinnati's lineup, played nearly every day without injury or rest, and provided Gold Glove defense in the outfield.

The Reds signed Pinson out of high school in Oakland, California (the same high school that earlier produced Frank Robinson and Curt Flood). After 2 outstanding minor league seasons, Pinson led the majors in runs (131) and doubles (47) as a rookie in 1959. For that season, he batted .316 (fourth in the National League) with 205 hits (second to Hank Aaron), 20 home runs and 84 RBIs. He finished second to Willie McCovey for National League Rookie of the Year in 1959.

Outstanding Feat

Between 1959 and 1967, Vada Pinson never played fewer than 154 games in a season.

120

Pinson's batting average slipped to .287 in 1960, and his 37 doubles, 10 fewer than the year before, were still the best in the majors. In 1961, Pinson hit a career high .343 to help the Reds win the National League pennant. He led the major leagues with 208 hits and won the Gold Glove for his work in center field.

Pinson drove in 100 or more runs in each of the next two years, leading the majors in hits (204) and triples (14) in 1963 while batting .313. (He would lead the majors in triples one more time, with 13 in 1967.) Though still respectable, Pinson's hitting statistics declined steadily at the end of the 1960s, and he was traded to the St. Louis Cardinals prior to the 1969 season for outfielder Bobby Tolan and pitcher Wayne Granger, 2 players who proved to be integral to the Reds' pennant-winning season of 1970.

Playing in St. Louis only 1 season, Pinson hit .255 with 10 home runs and 70 RBIs, and was traded to the Cleveland Indians for

Bats: Left   **Throws:** Left
Height: 5' 11"   **Weight:** 181 lb.

Born: August 11, 1938 in Memphis, TN
Debut: April 15, 1958
Final Game: September 28, 1975

outfielder Jose Cardenal. Pinson's power made something of a comeback for the Indians, as he hit .286 with 24 home runs and 82 RBIs in his inaugural American League season. But he never again approached that kind of performance during the rest of his career, which consisted of 2 seasons each with Cleveland, the California Angels, and the Kansas City Royals. He retired in 1976 after an 18-year career that saw Pinson amass over 2700 hits on a .286 career batting average.

Did You Know ...

At 2,757, Vada Pinson had more career hits than Hall of Famers Ted Williams, Billy Williams and Joe Morgan.

Top 5 Catchers of the 1960s

1 **Elston Howard** – A masterful handler of pitchers with a potent bat, Howard was a fixture at catcher for the Yankees in the early 1960s, hitting a combined .284 as the Yankees' everyday catcher from 1960 to 1966. He batted .348 in 1961, the second-highest batting average in the American League to Detroit's Norm Cash (.361), and hit .287 during his MVP season of 1963, catching 132 games and winning the first of his 2 Gold Glove awards.

2 **Joe Torre** – Torre was probably the best all-around catcher in the National League during the 1960s. Playing for the Braves from 1960 to 1968, Torre hit a combined .294 over that period, twice driving in more than 100 runs and hitting a career-high 36 home runs in 1966. Traded to the Cardinals before 1969, Torre eclipsed 100 RBIs in each of his first 3 seasons with St. Louis.

3 **Bill Freehan** – Freehan caught more than 100 games per year from 1964 through 1972, winning consecutive Gold Gloves from 1965 to 1969. A career-long Tiger, he hit .300 in 1964 while catching 141 games. His .993 fielding percentage is tied for third all-time among catchers.

4 **Earl Battey** – Signed by the White Sox, Battey was traded to the Washington Senators in 1960 and became the Twins' everyday catcher through the 1966 season. His best offensive season was 1962, with 26 home runs and 84 RBIs while batting .285. Battey won 3 Gold Gloves.

5 **John Roseboro** – Roseboro was the Dodgers' starting catcher from 1961 until he was traded to the Minnesota Twins before the 1967 season. A 3-time All-Star and winner of a pair of Gold Gloves, Roseboro was a .240 career hitter who best single-season average was .287 in 1964.

Tommy Harper
Seattle's Finest

One of the two American League expansion teams in 1969, the Seattle Pilots lasted one season before they disappeared from the great northwest and re-emerged in Milwaukee henceforth as the Brewers. There were few bright spots in the Pilots' lone season, though they did manage to avoid having the worst won-lost record in the league. (The Cleveland Indians' disastrous 1969 season deprived the Pilots of that dubious honor.)

Tommy Harper was a bright spot for Seattle in 1969. But that season was simply the culmination of a solid decade for Harper, and a hint at the kind of outstanding productivity still to come from Harper's quick bat and feet.

The Cincinnati Reds signed Harper in 1960 off the campus of San Francisco State University. After three seasons in the Reds' minor league system, Harper debuted in 1963 as a starting outfielder, hitting .260 with 12 stolen bases and 37 RBIs. By 1965, Harper had developed into a considerable offensive threat, batting .257 with 166 hits, 18 home runs, and 64 RBIs as the Reds' lead-off

Outstanding Feat

Tommy Harper's stolen-base championship in 1969 marked the only time a member of a first-year expansion team led the league in any offensive category.

hitter. Harper also stole 35 bases that year, and led the majors with 126 runs scored.

On the verge of stardom, Harper's offensive output dropped dramatically over the next 2 years, and the Reds traded him to Cleveland, where injuries limited his ability during the 1968

season, the worst statistically of his career. The Indians left the disappointing Harper unprotected, and he was acquired by Seattle in the league's expansion draft on October 15, 1968.

Harper had his best season in years for the lowly Pilots. At full strength finally, he led the American League in stolen bases with 73. As the Pilots' lead-off hitter, he scored 78 runs and drove in 41 himself. The next year, 1970, he moved with the team to Milwaukee, becoming one of the few players in major league history to hit more than 30 home runs and steal more than 30 bases in the same season. He also had career highs in RBIs (82) and batting average (.296). Harper went on to have productive years with the Boston Red Sox (including leading the league again in stolen bases with 54 in 1973) before retiring as a member of the Baltimore Orioles in 1976.

Bats: Right **Throws:** Right
Height: 5' 10" **Weight:** 168 lb.

Born: October 14, 1940 in Oak Grove, LA
Debut: April 9, 1962
Final Game: September 29, 1976

A solid ballplayer for 15 seasons, Harper can take pride in the fact that his offensive single-season records with the Seattle Pilots will never be broken. As Roger Maris and Maury Wills have proven, not even baseball titans such as Babe Ruth and Ty Cobb can make the same claim.

> *Did You Know ...*
>
> *With a total of 23, Tommy Harper is tied for fifteenth all-time in lead-off home runs with the Detroit Tigers' Lou Whittaker.*

Top 5 Shortstops of the 1960s

1 **Ernie Banks** – Banks was to redefine the power and run production standards for a shortstop, starting in 1955 when he hit .295 with 44 home runs and 117 RBIs. Throughout the 1960s, Banks remained a consistent offensive threat despite the fact that he played for mostly sub-.500 Cub teams. During the decade, first as the Chicago Cubs' shortstop and mostly as the team's first baseman, Banks averaged 27 home runs and 95 RBIs per season.

2 **Luis Aparicio** - Speed and defense made Aparicio the American League's premier shortstop from the mid-1950s to the mid-1960s. Starting in 1956, he led the league in stolen bases for 9 consecutive years, with a career high of 57 in 1964. An 11-time All-Star, Aparicio collected 2,677 hits on a career batting average of .262, with a total of 506 stolen bases.

3 **Maury Wills** - In addition to being an excellent shortstop (a 2-time Gold Glove winner), Wills was so good at stealing bases that he won the Most Valuable Player award in 1962 while leading the league in that offensive category and no other. He stole 104 bases that year, 8 better than Ty Cobb's single-season record. During his 14-season career, Wills averaged 49 steals per season, leading the league five different times.

4 **Bert Campaneris** –Campaneris came up with the Kansas City Athletics in 1964, hitting a home run in his first at-bat and 2 homers in his first game. Starting in 1965, he led the league in stolen bases in each of his first 4 seasons and in 6 out of his first 8 years with the A's.

5 **Dick Groat** - As the 1960 National League batting champion with a .325 average, Groat also led the league in singles (154), finished third in hits (186), and was sixth in on-base percentage (.371). He was voted league MVP for 1960.

Jim Kaat

This Kitty Did It All

Jim Kaat was one of the most amazing all-around athletes to toe a major league pitching rubber. He pitched in the majors for 25 years, was quite possibly the best fielding pitcher ever to play the game, and was one of baseball's best-hitting pitchers throughout his career.

He also happened to win enough games (283) to qualify for enshrinement in Cooperstown, though at this writing he was not yet a member of the Hall of Fame.

A teenage Kaat was signed by the Washington Senators in 1957, and joined the Senators' staff for keeps at the end of the 1960 season. He was part of the starting rotation during the team's first year in Minnesota in 1961, going 9-17 for the Twins despite a respectable 3.90 ERA. In 1962, Kaat went from a 17-game loser to an 18-game winner, finishing 18-14 for the Twins with a 3.14 ERA and leading the league with 5 shutouts. He won 17 games for the Twins in 1964 and 18 games as the Twins won the American

---

Outstanding Feat

When Jim Kaat pitched a league-leading 25 wins for the Minnesota Twins in 1966, he also led the majors in starts with 41, and led the American League in complete games (19) and innings pitched (304).

League pennant in 1965. He led the league with 42 starts that year.

Kaat's best season for the Twins came in 1966, when he went 25-13 with a 2.75 ERA. He won 16 games for the Twins in 1967, and 14 in each of the next 3 seasons. Kaat would not be a 20-game winner again until 1974 and 1975, when he won 21 and 20 games respectively for the Chicago White Sox.

As a batter, Kaat often helped his own cause, hitting .185 over his career with 16 home runs and 106 RBIs. As a fielder, Kaat had no peers among pitchers, and few major leaguers at any position fielded as well as he did. He won 16 consecutive Gold Gloves (matched only by Brooks Robinson)..

Bats: Left   **Throws:** Left
Height: 6' 4"   **Weight:** 217 lb.

Born: November 7, 1938 in Zeeland, MI
Debut: August 2, 1959
Final Game: July 1, 1983

Did You Know ...

Jim Kaat was the last member of the original Washington Senators to play in the major leagues, retiring in 1983.

Boog Powell
Big Man, Big Numbers

Once, after striking out, a disgusted Boog Powell slammed his bat to the ground and splintered it. He was that strong.

He could be just as devastating to rival pitchers as he was to uncooperative bats. In a 17-season big league career, Powell hit over 300 home runs and was integral to the Baltimore Orioles success in the late 1960s and early 1970s.

Signed by the Orioles in 1959, Powell joined the big league club for keeps as an outfield in 1962, hitting 15 home runs and driving in 53 runs in 124 games. His .606 slugging percentage led the American League in 1964. By 1966, he had moved full-time to first base, and helped the Orioles win the American League pennant (and was no doubt a factor in Frank Robinson's Triple Crown that year) by hitting .287 with 34 home runs and 109 RBIs. He was slowed by injuries in 1967, but rebounded in 1968 (22 home runs and 85 RBIs) and was outstanding in the Orioles' pennant-winning 1969 with 37 home runs and 121 RBIs while hitting a career-high .304.

Outstanding Feat

On August 16, 1966, Boog Powell hit 3 opposite-field home runs in a single game ... over the "Green Monster" in Boston's Fenway Park.

In 1970, Powell led the Orioles to the American League championship by hitting 35 home runs with 114 RBIs – good enough to win the Most Valuable Player award. In 17 big league seasons – 4 of them All-Star seasons – Powell hit 339 home runs and drove in over 1100 runs.

Bats: Left **Throws:** Right
Height: 6' 4" **Weight:** 240 lb.

Born: August 17, 1941 in Lakeland, FL
Debut: September 26, 1961
Final Game: August 24, 1977

Did You Know ...

Boog Powell won the American League's Most Valuable Player award in 1970 ... after finishing second in the MVP balloting to Harmon Killebrew the previous year.

Mel Stottlemyre

Old Reliable Youngster

Had he been born a decade earlier and pitched in his prime with the New York Yankee powerhouses of the 1950s and early 1960s, Mel Stottlemyre almost certainly would have accumulated Hall-of-Fame-worthy numbers by the end of his career. But it wasn't to be. As the Yankees' best starting pitcher in their late 1960s decline, Stottlemyre proved that his heart matched his talent. Unfortunately, the Yankees' support – and his numbers for that period – didn't match the effort and skills that Stottlemyre consistently brought to the mound.

A member of the Yankees' organization for his entire career, Stottlemyre was signed as a free agent in 1961. In 1964, he won 13 games for the Yankees' AAA Richmond club before being called up to the big leagues and making his debut on August 12, 1964. Over the course of the next 6 weeks, Stottlemyre went 9-3 with a 2.06 ERA as the Yankees won 22 out of 28 games in September to overcome the Chicago White Sox and clinch the American League pennant on the next-to-last day of the season. Stottlemyre was 1-1

Outstanding Feat

Mel Stottlemyre is the only Yankee pitcher since 1920 to win 20 or more games 3 times for non-pennant winners.

---

in the 1964 World Series, and he was chosen to start the decisive seventh game on only 2 days' rest. The Yankees lost that game 7-5, and Stottlemyre wasn't involved in the decision.

Stottlemyre wasn't an overpowering pitcher. He had excellent control and placement of his pitches, and threw "heavy" stuff that induced ground balls more than strikeouts. He was 20-9 in 1965 with a 2.93 ERA and led the American League in innings pitched with 291. In 1966, with a Yankees team that finished last in the American League, his record slipped to 12-20 though his ERA was still a respectable 3.80. It was the last time in the 1960s that Stottlemyre's ERA would exceed 3.00.

A 5-time All-Star, Stottlemyre pitched 250 or more innings in 9 consecutive seasons. He was a 20-game winner again in 1968 and 1969, leading the league in complete games with 24 in 1969. In 11 seasons with the Yankees, Stottlemyre won 164 games and posted a career ERA of 2.97. A torn rotator cuff abruptly ended his career in 1974.

Bats: Right **Throws:** Right
Height: 6' 2" **Weight:** 190 lb.

Born: November 13, 1941 in Hazleton, MO
Debut: August 12, 1964
Final Game: August 16, 1974

Bill Mazeroski

Second to None with a Glove

He was so good at his position that other players stopped what they were doing to watch him *practice*. He was an artist whose materials were horse-hide and leather. The keystone was his canvas.

You can't talk about the great second baseman unless you include the man who did it better and longer than just about anyone else. That was Bill Mazeroski.

With shortstop Dick Groat, Mazeroski turned the double play into his own private possession. Groat was a first-rate shortstop, but even after he moved on to St. Louis, Mazeroski would keep turning double plays with whoever would get him the ball. Winner of 8 Gold Gloves, Mazeroski holds more defensive records than any other player in major league history.

He also wasn't a bad hitter, finishing his 17-year career (all with Pittsburgh) with more than 2,000 hits and a .260 lifetime

Outstanding Feat

Bill Mazeroski is the only second baseman in major league history to have participated in more than 1700 double plays. (Nellie Fox's 1619 is second all-time to Maz's 1706.)

batting average. Of course, it wasn't his glove but his last at-bat in the 1960 World Series that made Maz a household name. Leading off in the bottom of the ninth in a 9-9 Game #7, Mazeroski sent a Ralph Terry fastball over the left-field fence to make the Pirates world champions and send Casey Stengel, ultimately, to the National League (as the fired Yankee manager reborn as the inaugural field manager of the expansion New York Mets).

It was the first World Series to end with a walk-away home run, and perhaps it was somewhat ironic that it wasn't one of the Pirates sluggers but their defensive whiz who torpedoed the Yankee juggernaut with one swing. However, it wasn't Mazeroski's only display of power. He hit as many as 19 home runs in a season (1958), and

Bats: Right   **Throws:** Right
Height: 5' 11"   **Weight:** 183 lb.

Born: September 5, 1936 in Wheeling, WV
Debut: July 7, 1956
Final Game: October 4, 1972
Inducted into the
Baseball Hall of Fame: 2001

finished his career with 138 homers, seventeenth all-time among second basemen ... none of whom could match him in the field.

Mazeroski retired 34 games into the 1972 season. He's fifth in Pirate history in games played (2,163), sixth in career at-bats with the team (7,755), and eighth in career hits (2,016). A 7-time All-Star, Mazeroski was elected to the Baseball Hall of Fame in 2001.

Pirate's Blast Scuttles Yankees

The First World Series Walk-Off

It was a World Series of improbabilities, played out as no one could have expected or predicted.

On the one hand you had the New York Yankees, the perennial October players, back in the World Series (their tenth appearance in the last 12 years) after a 1-year absence. The Yankees earned their World Series berth by sprinting ahead of the rest of the American League in September, winning their last 15 games.

For the Pittsburgh Pirates, it was their first World Series appearance since 1927.

In the first 6 games, the Yankees were clearly the dominant team (outscoring the Pirates 46-17), but had only 3 victories to show for it. Whitey Ford pitched shutouts for the Yankees in games 3 and 6. Vern Law, the Pirates' 20-game winner and the eventual Cy Young Award winner that year, claimed 2 of the Pirates' wins, while veteran left-hander Harvey Haddix posted 1 victory and a save.

Game 7 turned out to be one of the most exciting in World Series history.

Hal Smith
His 3-run home run in the eighth
inning pout the Pirates on top ...
temporarily.

Law retired the Yankees in order in the first 2 innings, while the Pirates scored 2 runs in each of the first 2 frames. The Yankees finally scored off Law in the fifth inning as Bill Skowron led off the inning with a solo home run to the right field seats. The Yankees scored 4 more runs in the sixth inning, off reliever Roy Face, who gave up an RBI single to Mickey Mantle and Yogi Berra's 3-run homer.

The game stayed 5-4 in favor of the Yankees until the top of the eighth inning, when back-to-back RBI hits by John Blanchard and Clete Boyer raised the Yankee lead to 7-4. But in the bottom of the eighth, the Pirates rallied for 5 runs – on singles by Dick Groat and Roberto Clemente and a 3-run homer by Hal Smith – to take a 9-7 lead into the ninth inning.

Bob Friend, an 18-game winner during the regular season, came in to close out the ninth. But he gave up back-to-back singles to Bobby

Harvey Haddix retired the Yankees in the top of the ninth inning after allowing the tying runs.

Richardson and Dale Long. So Pirates manager Danny Murtaugh brought in Haddix to pitch to Roger Maris, the American League MVP of 1960. Haddix got Maris to foul out, and then gave up an RBI single to Mantle. Berra grounded out to Rocky Nelson at first, scoring Gil McDougald from third (pinch running for Long). Then Skowron grounded out to end the inning with the score tied at 9.

In the bottom of the ninth, second baseman Bill Mazeroski led off for the Pirates. On deck was Dick Stuart, the team's leading home run hitter.

The Yankee pitcher was right-hander Ralph Terry, a 10-game winner for New York during the regular season. Terry had recorded the last out of the eighth inning, inducing Don Hoak to fly out. Hoak would be the last Pirate to make an out of the Series. Mazeroski took a strike on Terry's first pitch, and sent the second one over the left field wall at Forbes Field for a 10-9 Pirate victory.

It was the first walk-off home run in World Series history.

Bill Mazeroski's ninth-inning home run ended the 1960 World Series, and Casey Stengel's career as New York Yankees manager.

Top 5 Second Basemen of the 1960s

1 **Bill Mazeroski** - Winner of 8 Gold Gloves, Mazeroski holds more defensive records than any other player in major league history. He wasn't a bad hitter either, finishing his 17-year career (all with the Pittsburgh Pirates) with more than 2,000 hits and a .260 lifetime batting average.

2 **Bobby Richardson** - From 1961 through 1966, the durable Bobby Richardson never had fewer than 600 official at-bats in a season. He led the American League in hits in 1962 with 209, with a career-high .302 batting average. He was the league's Gold Glove second baseman from 1961 to 1965.

3 **Pete Runnels** - Pete Runnels was the 1960s' first two-time batting champion, and the first player ever to win two batting titles while playing two different positions. As the Boston Red Sox starting second baseman, Runnels won his first batting championship in 1960 with a .320 average. As the Red Sox first baseman in 1962, Runnels claimed his second batting title with a .326 average.

4 **Pete Rose** - Rose was signed by the Cincinnati Reds in 1960, and had become the team's starting second baseman by opening day of 1963. His best season during the 1960s came in 1968, when Rose led the league in hitting (.335), hits (210) and on-base percentage (.391. He repeated as the National League batting champion in 1969 (.348), the first year that he led the National League in runs scored (120).

5 **Rod Carew** – Rod Carew's Hall of Fame career began in the 1960s, and he won the first of his 7 batting titles by the end of the decade, hitting .332 in 1969. The 1967 Rookie of the Year hit .300 or better in 15 of the 19 seasons he played, finishing with a career average of .328 and 3,053 hits.

Ron Perranoski

What a Relief!

The 1960s were the decade when the relief specialist became an essential part of a winning team's pitching formula. While starting pitchers were still expected to complete the game they started, managers in the 1960s began to realize the efficiency of building the relief function around a dedicated closer.

For the Los Angeles Dodgers in the first half of the 1960s, that closer was a left-hander named Ron Perranoski. Signed off the Michigan State University campus by the Chicago Cubs, Perranoski was traded to the Dodgers in 1960. He made the Dodgers' squad in 1961, appearing in 53 games (only 1 a start, the only start of his career), and going 7-5 with 6 saves and a 2.65 ERA. Perranoski established himself as the Dodgers' closer in 1962, appearing in 70 games and finishing 39 of them, with 20 saves and a 2.85 ERA.

Outstanding Feat

In 1963, Ron Perranoski's 16 wins in relief tied him with Philadelphia's Jim Konstanty for the second highest total in a season. Roy Face set the record with 18 in 1959, a record that still stands.

In 1963, as the Dodgers went on to win the National League pennant and the World Series against the New York Yankees, Perranoski had a career year, with a 16-3 record and 21 saves with a 1.67 earned run average. He appeared only once in the World Series, shutting down the Yankees in the bottom of the 9th to earn a save in preserving a 4-1 victory for the Dodgers and Johnny

Podres. (Every other game was a complete-game victory for the Dodgers' starter.)

Over the next 4 years, Perranoski appeared in 256 games for the Dodgers, saving 54 while going 23-27 with a 2.73 ERA. He was traded to the Minnesota Twins following the 1967 season, and saved 65 games for the Twins over the next two years, leading the American League in that category both seasons. His performance tailed off sharply after that, and Perranoski retired in 1973 after 13 seasons with 179 career saves.

Bats: Left **Throws:** Left
Height: 6' 0" **Weight:** 192 lb.

Born: April 1, 1936 in Paterson, NJ
Debut: April 14, 1961
Final Game: June 17, 1973

Tony Oliva

Twin Hit Machine

Tony Oliva's impact on the American League was immediate. His outstanding rookie year of 1964 saw Oliva lead the American League in 5 different offensive categories: hits (217), runs (109), doubles (43), total bases (374) and batting average (.323). He was easily the American League Rookie of the Year, and finished fourth in Most Valuable Player balloting.

Oliva followed his great debut season by repeating as batting champion in 1965 with a .321 average. He also led the league again in hits, as he would do 2 more times in his career. Oliva won his third batting title in 1971, with a career-best .337 average.

Oliva spent all of his career with the Minnesota Twins. He seemed destined for a place in Cooperstown until knee injuries severely limited his hitting effectiveness. In 6 full seasons during the 1960s, Oliva hit a combined .308 with 1,087 hits. After he injured his knee in 1972, Oliva's numbers for the next 4 years were significantly lower: a .277 average with 446 hits.

Outstanding Feat

Tony Oliva's 374 total bases in 1964 are still tied for the major league record for a rookie (with Hal Trosky of the Cleveland Indians).

An 8-time All-Star, the Twins outfielder won his only Gold Glove in 1966.

Bats: Left   **Throws:** Right
Height: 6' 2"   **Weight:** 190 lb.

Born: July 20, 1938 in Pinar Del Rio, Cuba
Debut: September 9, 1962
Final Game: September 29, 1976

Did You Know ...

During their careers with the Minnesota Twins, Harmon Killebrew and Tony Oliva hit home runs in the same game 42 times.

Gary Peters

Southside Southpaw

During the heart of the 1960s, Gary Peters made up half of one of the most effective – and under-rewarded – righty-lefty pitching tandems in baseball.

Along with right-hander Joe Horlen, the left-handed Peters provided the White Sox with consistently strong starting pitching, with an outstanding combined ERA between 1963 and 1967 of 2.50. Yet he averaged only a little over 15 victories (76-49) due to consistently anemic run support from the White Sox. (Horlen fared even worse during that same 5-year period, going 66-49 on a 2.42 ERA.)

The lanky Peters was signed by the White Sox out of Grove City (Pennsylvania) College in 1956. He toiled in the White Sox organization until 1963, when he was named American League Rookie of the Year by going 19-8 with league-leading 2.33 ERA. He finished 4th in the league in strikeouts with 189.

Outstanding Feat

Never considered an overpowering pitcher, Gary Peters ranked fifth or better in the American League in strikeouts 3 times during his career, with his best single-season strikeout total coming in 1967 (215).

His numbers improved in 1964, as the White Sox finished 1 game behind the league-champion Yankees. Peters went 20-8 (tied with Dean Chance for the most victories among American League pitchers) with a 2.50 ERA, 4th best in the league. The workhorse of Chicago's staff, Peter finished among the top 5 in the league in starts (36), innings pitched (273) and strikeouts (205). Always a good hitting pitcher (career batting average of .222), Peters hit 4 home runs and knocked in 19 runs during the 1964 season.

During the next 5 years, Peters had only two winning seasons for the White Sox: 12-10 in 1966 with a league-best 1.98 ERA, and 16-11 in 1968 with a 2.28 ERA. In 1968-69, he had a combined 14-28 record for the White Sox. Following the 1969 season, the White Sox traded Peters to Boston, where he won 33 games before being released at the end of the 1972 season.

In 11 seasons with the White Sox, his 2.92 ERA was good for only a 91-78 record. The White Sox as a team never hit above .250 during the years when Peters was in their starting rotation. How many games could he have won with a better-hitting team?

Bats: Left **Throws:** Left
Height: 6' 2" **Weight:** 200 lb.

Born: April 21, 1937 in Grove City, PA
Debut: September 10, 1959
Final Game: September 23, 1972

Pete Runnels

The Anonymous Batting Champ

Pete Runnels may well be the least-known player in this book. Yet he was the 1960s' first two-time batting champion, and the first player in the modern era to win two batting titles while playing two different positions.

Runnels broke into the big leagues as a shortstop for the Washington Senators in 1951. Over the next 7 years, splitting his time between shortstop and second base, Runnels hit .274 for Washington, with a high mark of .310 in 1956. He was traded to the Red Sox before the 1958 season, when he hit .322, the second highest average in the league. He also registered a career high 183 hits in his first year with Boston, fourth best in the league.

As Boston's starting second baseman, Runnels won his first batting championship in 1960 with a .320 average. Runnels moved over to first base in 1961, hitting .317 that year. As the Red Sox first baseman in 1962, Runnels claimed his second batting title with a .326 average.

Outstanding Feat

In his 5 years with Boston, Pete Runnels was one of the league's most consistent hitters, with a combined average of .320 over that period.

146

That performance wasn't enough to keep Runnels in a Red Sox uniform, as he was traded in the off season to the Houston Colt 45's. Runnels hit only .253 in 1963, his only full season with Houston. He was released 22 games into the 1964 season, and never played again in the majors.

Bats: Left **Throws:** Right
Height: 6' 0" **Weight:** 170 lb.

Born: January 28, 1928 in Lufkin, TX
Debut: July 1, 1951
Final Game: May 14, 1964

Did You Know ...

Between Pete Runnels and Carl Yastrzemski, the Red Sox claimed half of the American League batting championships during the 1960s.

Steve Barber

Baltimore Clipper

Strong left-handed starting pitching was a characteristic of the Baltimore Orioles staff throughout the 1960s. For the first half of that decade, that banner was carried by Steve Barber.

Barber was signed by the Orioles in 1957. In 1960, he joined a strong Orioles staff as the only left-handed starter, going 10-7 with a 3.22 ERA in helping contribute to the Orioles' second-place finish. Barber also led the league in walks with 113.

Barber became the Orioles' ace in 1961 with an 18-12 record and a 3.33 ERA. He led the American League in shutouts with 8, and led the Orioles in starts (34) and innings pitched (248). Injuries limited Barber to a 9-6 record in 1962, but he bounced back in 1963 with his best season, going 20-13 with a 2.75 ERA and a career-high 180 strikeouts.

Outstanding Feat

Steve Barber set the Orioles record for shutouts in a season with 8 in 1961. That mark was eclipsed in 1975 when Jim Palmer pitched 10 shutouts.

During the next 3 years, Barber won 34 games for the Orioles. He was traded to the New York Yankees after the start of the 1967 season. He pitched for 5 more teams over the next 7 years, retiring in 1974 with a career record of 121-106 and a career ERA of 3.36.

From 1960 to 1966, Barber was one of the best left-handers in the American League, winning 91 games with a 3.07 ERA. He pitched in 2 All-Star games.

Bats: Left **Throws:** Left
Height: 6' 0" **Weight:** 200 lb.

Born: February 22, 1938 in Takoma Park, MD
Debut: April 21, 1960
Final Game: July 31, 1974

Did You Know ...

Steve Barber still ranks seventh all-time among Baltimore pitchers with 918 strikeouts in an Oriole uniform.

Mike McCormick

Savvy Southpaw

Mike McCormick never really lived up to the promise of his youth, when he was signed by the New York Giants as a "bonus baby" in 1956 and led the National League in ERA by age 21. But when it seemed that his career was ready to fade into the sunset, he made a remarkable comeback that made him the first National League Cy Young award winner.

McCormick went from the sand lots to the big league Giants without the benefit of minor league seasoning. He became a member of the Giants' starting rotation in 1958, winning 11 games that year and 12 the next. In 1960, pitching for the fifth-place San

---

Outstanding Feat

Mike McCormick was only 17 when he joined the Giants as one the most celebrated pitchers in American Legion baseball history with a 49-4 record.

150

Francisco Giants, McCormick won 15 games and led the National League with a 2.70 ERA.

He slipped to 13-16 in 1961 (with a 3.20 ERA), and during the Giants' pennant-winning season of 1962, arm problems caused McCormick to become the forgotten man on a strong pitching roster. He finished that year 5-5 with a 5.38 ERA in only 15 starts. That winter, the Giants shipped McCormick (along with reliever Stu Miller and catcher John Orsino) to the Baltimore Orioles for catcher Jimmie Coker and pitchers Jack Fisher and Billy Hoeft.

The Orioles were no doubt hoping that McCormick would regain his 1960 form, but it wasn't to be. During his 2 years in Baltimore, McCormick' arm troubles continued as he went a combined 6-10 with

Bats: Left **Throws:** Left
Height: 6' 2" **Weight:** 195 lb.

Born: September 29, 1938 in Pasadena, CA
Debut: September 3, 1956
Final Game: May 22, 1971

a 4.40 ERA in only 29 appearances (23 starts). Just prior to the 1965 season, Baltimore traded McCormick to the Washington Senators for a minor leaguer and cash. In 2 seasons with the Senators, McCormick went 19-22 with a 3.42 ERA.

The Giants re-acquired McCormick prior to the 1967 season, and it turned out to be a smart acquisition. McCormick led the league with a 22-10 record. He tossed 5 shutouts and posted a 2.85 ERA. He became the first National League Cy Young pitcher.

(Prior to 1967, only one Cy Young award was made to the best *major league* pitcher.)

McCormick never matched that performance again, going 23-23 for the Giants over the next 2 years. He retired in 1971 with a 134-128 record and a career ERA of 3.73.

Did You Know ...

An All-Star in 1960 and 1961, Mike McCormick was not named to the 1967 All-Star team – even though he ended up winning the National League Cy Young award that year.

Top 5 Managers of the 1960s

1 **Gil Hodges** - One of the great sluggers of the 1950s, Gil Hodges pulled off one of the most improbable managerial success stories when he led the New York Mets to their "miracle" championship in 1969. After a distinguished playing career for the Brooklyn/Los Angeles Dodgers and, for the final 1½ seasons, with the New York Mets, Hodges was traded by the Mets to the Washington Senators in 1963 specifically to be Washington's manager. In his first 4 seasons as Washington's skipper, Hodges's team improved gradually, yet finished among the American League's bottom 3 teams for all 4 of those seasons. Then the Senators finished a franchise-record sixth in 1967.

In 1968, manager Hodges was traded back to the Mets for pitcher Bill Denehy and $100,000. In his first season guiding the Mets, he led the team to a club record 73 wins in 1968. The miracle year was 1969, when his Mets leapt from near-mediocrity to world champions, winning 100 regular-season games and taking the World Series in 5 games against the Baltimore Orioles.

Hodges never made it back to the Series. The Mets won 83 games in both 1970 and 1971, and just before the start of the 1972 season, Hodges died from a heart attack. He was only 47.

2 **Walter Alston** – Walter Alston was the Dodgers' only manager throughout the 1960s. In fact, he was the team's manager for 23 years, from 1954 (in Brooklyn) to 1976 (in Los Angeles). His Dodgers won 3 National League pennants and 2 World Series during the 1960s. Altogether, Alston's teams won 7 pennants and 4 World

153

Series titles, and his teams finished in third place or higher in 17 of his 23 seasons.

There was no "typical" Alston club. The Dodgers of the 1950s were the best slugging team in baseball. The Dodgers of the 1960s were a low-scoring team that won consistently on pitching and defense. He was named Manager of the Year 6 times, and was elected to the Baseball Hall of Fame in 1983.

3 Ralph Houk – Probably no other manager in major league history found more success faster than Ralph Houk during his first tour as New York Yankees skipper. As a player, Houk appeared in only 91 games over 8 years with the Yankees, posting a career batting average of .272.

Following the 1960 World Series loss to the Pittsburgh Pirates, the Yankees let go of manager Casey Stengel after 12 seasons at the helm of the Yankees' 1950s dynasty. Houk replaced him, and couldn't have done better in the job, leading the Yankees to World Series championships in 1961 and 1962 and a third American League pennant in 1963.

Houk moved up to the general manager's office for the next 2-plus years, only to return as Yankee field skipper midway through 1966, replacing Johnny Keane. He remained the Yankee manager through the 1973 season, though he never achieved the same level of success he experienced during his first round as manager (his best finish was second in the Eastern Division in 1970, with 93 victories).

After leaving the Yankees, Houk took turns managing the Detroit Tigers and Boston Red Sox for 5 seasons each. His only championship teams came during those first 3 years with the Yankees.

4 **Red Schoendienst** – A Hall of Fame second baseman for the St. Louis Cardinals, New York Giants and Milwaukee Braves, Red Schoendienst spent 14 years as the Cardinals' manager, leading the team to pennants in 1967 and 1968, with a World Series championship in 1967. The Cards won over 1,000 with Schoendienst at the helm.

5 **Dick Williams** – Dick Williams managed only 3 seasons during the 1960s, but his impact as a field leader was immediate, and indicative of the Hall of Fame career that was to come. (Williams was elected to the Baseball Hall of Fame in 2008.)

After a 13-year playing career with 5 teams (including 3 tours with the Baltimore Orioles), Williams was named manager of the Boston Red Sox prior to the 1967 season. The 1960s had not been kind to the Bosox. From 1960 through 1966, the team's best finish had been sixth place. During the other 6 seasons, the team finished seventh, eighth and ninth twice each.

Williams' tough love approach to managing produced an American League pennant for Boston in 1967 after a 41-year drought. The next 2 seasons, Boston finished fourth and third respectively under Williams' guidance. He was let go by the Red Sox, and went on to manage 5 other teams, winning World Series titles in 1972 and 1973 with the Oakland Athletics.

Tony Conigliaro

Slugger Down

With acknowledgement of the fatal pitch that felled Cleveland Indians shortstop Ray Chapman in 1920, the next most devastating bean ball in major league history was delivered on August 18, 1967.

The victim of that fastball was Tony Conigliaro, a phenomenal young slugger whose career was tragically derailed that August evening.

Conigliaro was signed in 1962 by the Boston Red Sox at age 17. Two years later, he was the starting right fielder for the Bosox. He hit .290 with 54 RBIs that season. He also set major league records for a teenager with 24 home runs and a .530 slugging average.

The next year, Conigliaro was even better. His 32 home runs were tops in the American League in 1965, making Conigliaro the youngest player ever (at age 20) to win the home run crown. He followed in 1966 with 28 home runs and 93 RBIs, establishing him one of the league's most feared sluggers by age 21.

Outstanding Feat

On opening day for 1969, Tony Conigliaro celebrated his return to the Boston Red Sox lineup by homering in that game.

In 1967, Conigliaro picked up where he left off the previous year. By mid-August, only 95 games into the season, he already had 20 home runs and 67 RBIs (with a .287 batting average and .519 slugging percentage) when he was struck in the face by a pitched ball. He was carried off the field on a stretcher, sustaining a broken cheekbone and severe damage to his left retina. Largely as a result of his injuries, the major leagues adopted the style of batting helmet with the protective ear flap that is standard today.

Because of persisting problems with his vision, Conigliaro didn't play again until 1969. He hit 20 home runs with 82 RBIs during his "Comeback Player of the Year" season in 1969, and actually recorded his career-best power numbers in 1970 with 36 home runs and 116 RBIs. But permanent damage to his eyesight

Bats: Right   **Throws:** Right
Height: 6' 3"   **Weight:** 185 lb.

Born: January 7, 1945 in Revere, MA
Debut: April 16, 1964
Final Game: June 12, 1975

limited his playing ability thereafter. He was traded to the California Angels prior to the 1971 season, when he hit only 4 home runs in 74 games. He attempted another comeback with the Red Sox in 1975, but his career was over by age 30.

Did You Know ...

In 1990, the Boston Red Sox instituted The Tony Conigliaro Award to honor the memory of Tony Conigliaro (he passed away that year after suffering a heart attack and stroke in 1982). The award is made annually to the player who best overcomes an obstacle and adversity through the attributes of spirit, determination and courage.

Joe Horlen

Baseball's Best .500 Pitcher?

Every era of major league baseball seems to have a pitcher whose numbers are outstanding except where it matters most to Cooperstown: in the won-lost columns. Whether it's a Bert Blyleven (287-250) in the 1970s and 1980s or a Tim Belcher (146-140) in the 1990s, these are pitchers with great stuff who, on their best days, are absolutely unhittable – but in the end, they're basically .500 pitchers, a fact that, more often than not, is more of an indication of the caliber of teams they played for rather than their pitching prowess.

In the pitching-rich 1960s, no one had a more impressive yet frustrating career than Joe Horlen. Signed by the Chicago White Sox off the campus of Oklahoma State University in 1959, the right hander made his debut with the big league club at the end of 1961, going 1-3 in 4 starts. By 1963, Horlen was a regular in the starting rotation, going 11-7 with a 3.27 ERA.

Outstanding Feat

Joe Horlen pitched a no-hitter against the Detroit Tigers on September 10, 1967. That season he averaged less than 7 hits per 9 innings pitched.

Over the next 5 seasons, Horlen didn't post an ERA above 2.88, yet during that period his won-lost record was only 67-56, with a combined ERA of 2.34. He had a winning record in only one of those seasons: 1967, when Horlen went 19-7 with a league-leading 2.06 ERA. He was tops in the major leagues with 6 shutouts. That same year, he

finished second in the Cy Young voting to Boston's Jim Lonborg. It was his last winning season.

During those 5 seasons from 1964 to 1968, the White Sox as a team never hit higher than .247 (1964).

Horlen pitched for the White Sox through 1971, and was released following an 8-9 campaign. He signed with the Oakland A's and pitched mostly in relief in 1972, going 3-4 with a respectable ERA of 3.00. But Oakland released him at the end of the season, and no other team signed him. Horlen was out of baseball at age 34.

Bats: Right **Throws:** Right
Height: 6' 0" **Weight:** 175 lb.

Born: August 14, 1937 in San Antonio, TX
Debut: September 4, 1961
Final Game: October 4, 1972

For the 9 years he played during the 1960s (1961-1969), Horlen's 2.83 ERA was better than the earned run averages of Cy Young award winners Vern Law and Denny McLain, and lower than the ERAs of Hall of Famers such as Jim Bunning and Gaylord Perry. But his efforts returned only a 99-88 record, with a single All-Star appearance (1967).

Luis Tiant

Smoking Cigars and A.L. Hitters

You would never mistake Luis Tiant for any other pitcher in baseball. From his unique pitching style that often included turning his back to the batter, to his "Fu Manchu" moustache, to his smoking victory cigars in the shower, Tiant was truly one of a kind. He was also, at his best, one heck of a pitcher.

Tiant's most productive years came in the 1970s, when he won 15 or more games each year for the Boston Red Sox from 1972 through 1976 (including a trio of 20-win seasons). But he also pitched consistently well for the Cleveland Indians in the 1960s, including one year (1968) when he recorded the lowest earned run average by an American League pitcher since 1919 (when Walter Johnson posted a 1.49 ERA for the Washington Senators).

The Indians purchased Tiant from the Mexico City Tigers in 1962. He won 36 games in 2-plus seasons in the Indians' farm system. In 1964, he was called up to the Tribe after going 15-1 for their top minor league affiliate, Portland, striking out 154 batters

Outstanding Feat

On July 3, 1968, Luis Tiant struck out 19 Minnesota Twins in pitching a 10-inning, 1-0 shutout.

160

in 137 innings. Making his debut in the big leagues on July 19, 1964, he proved quickly that his performance at Portland was no fluke, going 10-4 for Cleveland the rest of that season with a 2.83 ERA.

The next 3 years Tiant went 35-31 with a 3.03 ERA, striking out an average of 8.2 batters per 9 innings pitched. Had he played for better Cleveland teams, Tiant should have won more games. And when Cleveland had its best showing in the 1960s, finishing third in 1968, Tiant turned in an outstanding season. He went 21-9, leading the American League in shutouts (9) and ERA (1.60), allowing only 5.3 hits for every 9 innings pitched. He was the starter (and loser) in a 1-0 All-Star Game, which turned out to be a fitting symbol for the "Year of the Pitcher" in 1968, as the game's only run was unearned.

Cleveland's strong showing in 1968 was followed by the team's total collapse in 1969, finishing with the worst record in the American League. Likewise, Tiant's numbers slid from his masterpiece season of 1968, as

Bats: Right **Throws:** Right

Height: 5' 11" **Weight:** 190 lb.

Born: November 23, 1940 in Marianao, Cuba

Debut: July 19, 1964

Final Game: September 4, 1982

he went from 20-game winner to 20-game loser, finishing 9-20, though with a respectable 3.71 ERA. Following the 1969 season, Tiant was traded to the Minnesota Twins in the deal that brought Dean Chance and Graig Nettles to the Indians.

Tiant struggled in Minnesota, due partly to injuries, and was released by the Twins in 1971 (and by the Atlanta Braves that same year) prior to his resurrection in Boston. During the 1960s, pitching for mostly lackluster Cleveland teams, Tiant won 75 games in 6 years with a fine 2.84 combined ERA. A 3-time All-Star, he retired in 1982 after winning 229 games.

Pete Rose

First Gear in the Big Red Machine

The accomplished and controversial career of Pete Rose extended well beyond the 1960s. But the greatest hitter not in the Hall of Fame collected the first of his 4,000 hits during the 1960s, and ended that decade on the verge of becoming the leader of the 1970s winningest team.

Cincinnati born and raised, Rose was signed by the Reds in 1960, and had become the Reds' starting second baseman by opening day of 1963. A strong debut season (.273 batting average on 170 hits) earned him Rookie of the Year honors for 1963. His best season during the 1960s came in 1968, when Rose led the league in hitting (.335), hits (210) and on-base percentage (.391), finishing second in the league in doubles (42) and second in the Most Valuable Player balloting to St. Louis Cardinals pitcher Bob Gibson.

Outstanding Feat

Pete Rose owns the major leagues' second longest hitting streak (44 games in 1978). He also holds the records for consecutive seasons with 100 or more hits – with 23.

60 From The '60s

During the 1960s, he led the league in hits twice, in 1965 (209) and in 1968 (210). He repeated as the National League batting champion in 1969 (.348), the first year that he led the National League in runs scored (120). He appeared in 4 All-Star games during the 1960s, and played in 17 All-Star games throughout his career.

During his playing career (which lasted until 1986), Rose won 3 batting titles and led the National League in hits 7 times. He also led the league in doubles 5 times and in runs scored 4 times. He was the National League's Most Valuable Player in 1973.

Bats: Both **Throws:** Right
Height: 5' 11" **Weight:** 200 lb.

Born: April 14, 1941 in Cincinnati, OH
Debut: April 8, 1963
Final Game: August 17, 1986

Rose retired having played more major league games (3,562) than anyone else. He's also the all-time leader in at-bats (14,053) and, of course, in hits (4,256).

Did You Know ...

Though remembered for his hitting, Pete Rose also won 2 Gold Gloves, in 1969 and 1970.

Jim Perry

Big Brother

No pair of pitching brothers has more combined strikeouts (5,110), shutouts (85) and Cy Young awards (3) than Jim and Gaylord Perry. Their combined 519 major league victories are second only to Phil and Joe Niekro (who won 539 games between them).

Older brother Jim broke into the majors in 1959 with the Cleveland Indians, going 12-10 with a 2.65 ERA as a starter and reliever. He was second in the Rookie of the Year balloting to the Washington Senators' Bob Allison. He started the 1960s by leading the American League in victories (18, tied with the Baltimore Orioles' Chuck Estrada), games started (36) and shutouts (4). In the next 2 years, pitching for a weak Cleveland team, Perry went 22-29, and was traded to the Minnesota Twins for pitcher Jack Kralick.

Outstanding Feat

Talk about loyalty: During the Minnesota Twins' 1965 pennant drive, Jim Perry won 7 straight games – all for a team that, earlier in the year, had put him on waivers!

60 From The '60s

Perry spent the next 5 years with the Twins shuttling between the bullpen and the starting rotation. Despite posting consistently solid ERAs, the most games he won for the Twins came during their pennant-winning season of 1965, when Perry went 12-7 with a 2.63 ERA.

His career seemed locked in mediocrity until Billy Martin was appointed as the Twins manager for 1969. Martin promptly made Perry his #1 starter. Perry responded with his first 20-victory season, going 20-6 with a 2.82 ERA and leading the Twins to a division championship. He topped that performance in 1970 with a 24-12 season that earned him the American League Cy Young award. He remained a durable starter for Minnesota, and later for Detroit and Cleveland, before retiring in 1975.

A 3-time All-Star, Perry was also

Bats: Both **Throws:** Right

Height: 6' 4" **Weight:** 200 lb.

Born: October 30, 1935 in Williamston, NC
Debut: April 23, 1959
Final Game: August 5, 1975

a good hitting pitcher, batting .199 over his 17-year career with 5 home runs and 59 RBIs. He finished his career with 32 shutouts.

Did You Know ...

In 1970, when Jim Perry won 24 games for the Minnesota Twins and Gaylord Perry won 23 games for the San Francisco Giants, the brothers pitched against each other in that year's All-Star game – a first for major league baseball.

Jimmy Wynn

Cannon Power

The early Houston teams (first they were the Colts, then the Astros) were easy to overlook. They weren't the worst of the expansion teams (the Mets owned that brand). And for most of the 1960s, they were best known for their domed stadium (baseball's first).

While the early Colts/Astros featured a handful of outstanding pitchers, their best-known player was an outfielder nicknamed "The Toy Cannon." Jimmy Wynn was a compact power-hitting centerfielder playing in a stadium that was not power-hitter friendly. Wynn was selected from the Cincinnati Reds' organization in the 1962 expansion draft, and debuted with Houston in 1963. He was a regular starter by 1965, when he led the team in hitting (.275), home runs (22), RBIs (73) and stolen bases (43). He was Houston's leading home run hitter for 6 straight seasons (1965 to 1970).

Outstanding Feat

In 1969, Jimmy Wynn set the National League record for walks with 148 ... a record topped 4 times since then by Barry Bonds.

Wynn's best season was 1967, when he finished second in the league in home runs (37) and fourth in RBIs (107), both career highs. He hit more than 30 home runs in a season 2 more times, in 1969 for the Astros and in 1974 for the Los Angeles Dodgers.

Bats: Right **Throws**: Right
Height: 5' 9" **Weight**: 170 lb.

Born: March 12, 1942 in Hamilton, OH
Debut: July 10, 1963
Final Game: September 27, 1977

Wynn finished with 291 career home runs. He remains third all-time in home runs (223) and RBIs (719) among Houston hitters.

Did You Know ...

Jimmy Wynn is tied for second all-time for the number of times hitting a home run in a 1-0 game ... with 4. Ted Williams leads the pack with 5.

Roy Face

Saving Bucs

The Pittsburgh Pirates' march to the National League pennant in 1960 was driven by solid pitching throughout the season. The team featured four dependable starters in Vern Law (the Cy Young winner at 20-9), Bob Friend (18-12), Vinegar Bend Mizell (13-5) and Harvey Haddix (11-10), a rotation that completed its starts in nearly half of the team's victories (47 complete games in 95 wins). The bullpen for the 1960 Pirates was equally effective, registering 33 saves, second-highest in the league to Cincinnati's 35. (These save totals may seem modest compared to the number of saves recorded today, but when was the last time you remember a major league team finishing with 47 complete games in a season – and that wasn't even the best in the National League?)

The leader of that bullpen was Roy Face, a diminutive pitcher with a wicked split-fingered fastball (known then as a forkball). Face was a spot starter and reliever when he joined the Pirates to

Outstanding Feat

The 22 consecutive wins posted by Roy Face in 1958-1959 represent the second longest winning streak by one pitcher in major league history (Carl Hubbell is first with 24).

168

stay in 1955. He led the league in appearances (68) in 1956 and in saves (20) in 1958. His career season came in 1959, when Face set the major league record for winning percentage (.947) on an 18-1 record.

The year the Pirates won the pennant, Face went 10-8 with 24 saves and a 2.90 ERA on a league-leading total of 68 appearances. He led the league again in saves in both 1961 (17) and 1962 (28). In 1962, he also had the lowest ERA of his career (1.88). Face continued pitching for Pittsburgh through the 1967 season, and pitched for Detroit and Montreal before retiring toward the end of the 1969 season.

In his 16-year career, Face posted a respectable 3.48 ERA while accumulating 193 saves pitching in 848 games.

Bats: Right **Throws:** Right
Height: 5' 8" **Weight:** 155 lb.

Born: February 20, 1928 in Stephentown, NY
Debut: April 16, 1953
Final Game: August 15, 1969

Did You Know ...

When Roy Face retired after the 1969 season, he ranked second in career saves (to Hoyt Wilhelm). Currently, he ranks thirty-eighth on the all-time career saves list.

Zoilo Versalles

Most Valuable Twin

Sometimes timing *is* everything. Have a career year for a perennial second-division team that rises to American League champion and you too could win a Most Valuable Player award. Just ask Zoilo Versalles.

The Minnesota Twins shortstop was clearly the team leader when the 1965 American League pennant arrived in the Twin Cities. The 5-foot-10 Cuban-born Versalles led the American League in at-bats (666), runs (126), doubles (45), triples (12), and total bases (308) while batting .273 with 19 home runs and 77 RBIs and winning the Golden Glove (his second).

He continued his clutch hitting in the World Series, which the Los Angeles Dodgers took 4 games to 3. Versalles hit .286 with 4 RBIs on 8 hits, including a double, a triple and a home run.

Outstanding Feat

From 1963 through 1965, Zoilo Versalles was the only American League player with double-figure totals in doubles, triples and home runs.

Versalles was signed by the Washington Senators in 1958 and made the major league club for keeps in 1960, the team's last year in the nation's capital. A lifetime .242 hitter, Versalles led the league in triples 3 times, and was never more productive at the plate than he was during his MVP season.

Bats: Right **Throws:** Right
Height: 5' 10" **Weight:** 150 lb.

Born: December 18, 1939 in Veldado, Cuba
Debut: August 1, 1959
Final Game: September 28, 1971

Did You Know ...

The 77 RBIs by Zoilo Versalles in 1965 were fourth best on the pennant-winning Minnesota Twins – but no one on that club had as many as 100. Versalles' RBI total was 2 better than Harmon Killebrew.

Dick Stuart

Bat Full of Runs, Fingers of Stone

Dick Stuart was the epitome of the good-hit, no-field first baseman. For nearly a decade in the big leagues, he was one of the game's most feared run producers, and a major liability in the field. If a player was ever made to be a designated hitter, it was Stuart. But he retired 7 seasons before the American League adopted the DH.

Stuart was signed by the Pittsburgh Pirates in 1951, and toiled in the Pirates' minor league organization until his major league in debut in 1958. He was a hitting terror in the minors, ripping 115 home runs in 1956 and 1957. In 67 games with the Pirates during his rookie season, Stuart hit .268 with 16 home runs and 48 RBIs. He posted a .543 slugging percentage. Stuart also had 1 error for every 4 games he played at first base, leading all National League first basemen in total errors despite playing only 64 games at first.

His best year for the Pirates was 1961, hitting .301 with 35 home runs and 117 RBIs. He finished fifth in the league in

Outstanding Feat

In 1963, when he socked 42 home runs for the Boston Red Sox, Dick Stuart became the first player in major league history to hit 30 or more home runs in each league (he hit 35 for Pittsburgh in 1961).

slugging that year with a .581 average. When his offensive numbers dipped dramatically in 1962 (.228 with 16 home runs and 64 RBIs), Stuart and pitcher Jack Lamabe were traded to the Boston Red Sox for catcher Jim Pagliaroni and pitcher Don Schwall.

A powerful pull hitter, Stuart's swing was made for the "Green Monster" in Fenway Park. He had a career season for Boston in 1963, hitting 42 home runs and leading the American League in RBIs (118) and total bases (319). He also set the major league record with 29 errors at first base. Stuart's numbers the next year were almost as good, as he hit 33 home runs and finished second in the league in RBIs with 114 (Brooks Robinson led with 118).

At his peak from 1961 to 1964, Stuart averaged 31 home runs and 103 RBIs per season. He also made every

Bats: Right **Throws:** Right
Height: 6' 4" **Weight:** 212 lb.

Born: November 7, 1932 in San Francisco, CA
Debut: July 10, 1958
Final Game: May 27, 1969

ground ball an adventure at first base, earning him the nicknames "Dr. Strangeglove."

After the 1964 season, the Red Sox traded Stuart to the Philadelphia Phillies for pitcher Dennis Bennett. Stuart spent 1 season with the Phillies, hitting 28 home runs and driving in 95 RBIs. He split the next season between the New York Mets and Los Angeles Dodgers, and then spent 2 years playing in Japan, closing out his career with the California Angels in 1969.

Hoyt Wilhelm

The Man with the Fantastic Flutter

It's probably the most unhittable pitch in baseball (with apologies to any pitch ever thrown by Sandy Koufax). And it may be the most unpitchable.

The knuckleball is slow, it doesn't rotate, and it doesn't offer many clues as to where it will end up. But one pitcher, more than any, is associated with the knuckleball, and was such a master of its unpredictability that it floated him all the way to Cooperstown.

Hoyt Wilhelm broke into the major leagues with the New York Giants in 1952 – as a 29-year-old rookie. That year he led the National League in winning percentage (.833 on a 15-3 record), in games pitched (71, all in relief) and in earned run average (2.43). For more than 2 decades thereafter, he remained one of the game's most durable and productive relievers.

Outstanding Feat

In his first major league at-bat, Hoyt Wilhelm hit a home run (the only one of his career). In his first major league start, he pitched a no-hitter.

Wilhelm entered the 1960s in the middle of a 5-year stretch with the Baltimore Orioles. After a brief stint as a starter for the Orioles, Wilhelm recorded 33 saves over the next 2 years (second best in the American League to Luis Arroyo's 36). Then he was traded to the White Sox in the deal that brought Luis Aparicio to the Orioles. In 6 years with Chicago, Wilhelm appeared in 361 games for the White Sox, all but 3 as a reliever. He saved 98

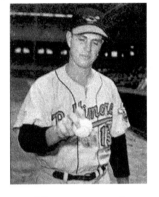

games, with an ERA of 1.92 for the 6 years combined.

Wilhelm closed out the 1960s by splitting the 1969 season between the California Angels and the Atlanta Braves, with a total of 14 saves and a combined ERA of 2.19.

Throughout the 1960s, no relief pitcher was as consistently effective as Wilhelm. During those 10 years, he won 75 games and saved 152 more, with an ERA of 2.19 for the decade. His career lasted 2 years beyond the 1960s, with his retirement after the 1971 season at age 48. His 1,070 career appearances were the major league record at the time Wilhelm called it quits.

Today he still ranks fifth in most career games by a pitcher. He remains the all-time major league leader in career wins in relief

Bats: Right **Throws:** Right
Height: 6' 0" **Weight:** 195 lb.

Born: July 26, 1922 in Huntersville, NC
Debut: April 19, 1952
Final Game: July 10, 1972
Inducted into the
Baseball Hall of Fame: 1985

(124) and career innings pitched in relief (1,871). An 8-time All-Star, Wilhelm was elected to the Baseball Hall of Fame in 1985.

Dick Allen

Power Unleashed

Some sluggers naturally inspire fear in opposing pitchers. Dick Allen was one of those.

In a 15-year career, Allen hit over 350 home runs with more than 1,100 RBIs. And while his best single season statistically was with the Chicago White Sox in 1972 (.308 batting average while leading the American League with both 37 home runs and 113 RBIs), Allen was most feared during the 1960s when he was a member of the Philadelphia Phillies.

Allen was signed by the Phillies in 1960 and joined the team full-time for the 1964 season. He won Rookie of the Year honors that year, leading the major leagues in runs (125) and triples (13) while batting .318 with 201 hits, 29 home runs and 91 RBIs.

In 1966, Allen hit 40 home runs with 110 RBIs and a .317 batting average, his best all-around year with the Phillies. He also led the league in slugging in 1966 with a .632 average. Allen was a

Outstanding Feat

Dick Allen's outstanding rookie season in 1964 included a new National League record for total bases by a rookie (352).

consistent threat as Philadelphia's All-Star third baseman during the 1960s, averaging 29 home runs and 90 RBIs per season from 1964 to 1969, and batting a combined .300 over that period.

Allen started the 1970s with the St. Louis Cardinals, and bounced from there to the Los Angeles Dodgers, and

Bats: Right **Throws:** Right
Height: 5' 11" **Weight:** 190 lb.

Born: March 8, 1942 in Wampum, PA
Debut: September 3, 1963
Final Game: June 19, 1977

then to the Chicago White Sox (for 3 seasons) before returning to Philadelphia and closing out his career with Oakland. He was named the American League's Most Valuable Player in 1972.

Did You Know ...

Dick played an indirect role in the demise of the reserve clause that bound players to their teams for life. His trade from the Philadelphia Phillies to the St. Louis Cardinals involved outfielder Curt Flood, whose refusal to report to Philadelphia set into motion the legal machinery that eventually led to the establishment of free agency in the mid-1970s.

Tom Seaver

Terrific, Even Miraculous

When the New York Mets lost a modern-day record 120 games in their inaugural season of 1962, it would have been hard to find even a die-hard fan who would genuinely imagine a championship season for the Mets … *ever*, let alone by the end of the decade. Yet the Mets did the miraculous in 1969, as the team was carried to the World Series on 2 young arms: the left one belonging to Jerry Koosman, the right one to Tom Seaver.

A highly recruited high school pitcher, Seaver signed with the Mets in 1966 and joined the big league club for good after a single season of minor league ball. He was the National League Rookie of the Year in 1967, going 16-13 as the first bona fide Mets pitching ace. The next year Seaver again won 16 games, posting a 2.20 ERA with 5 shutouts and 205 strikeouts. His achievement that year was

Outstanding Feat

During the "miracle" season of 1969, Tom Seaver nearly pitched a perfect game. On July 9 against the Chicago Cubs, Seaver pitched 8.1 perfect innings before giving up a double to Jim Qualls. Seaver won the game 4-0, striking out 11. It was his fourteenth victory of the season.

somewhat overshadowed by fellow Mets pitcher Jerry Koosman, who went 19-12 in his rookie year with a 2.08 ERA and 7 shutouts. While fans debated which of the young Mets aces was the better pitcher, most agreed that the Seaver-Koosman tandem provided the pitching foundation for a genuine Mets contender.

Contend they did, and then some. Led by a Cy Young season from Seaver, the "Miracle Mets" won the East Division by 8 games (thanks to the Chicago Cubs' collapse), swept the Atlanta Braves in the league championship series, and then beat the heavily favored Baltimore Orioles in 5 games to capture the decade's last World Series.

Bats: Right   **Throws:** Right
Height: 6' 1"   **Weight:** 206 lb.

Born: November 17, 1944 in Fresno, CA
Debut: April 13, 1967
Final Game: September 19, 1986
Inducted into the
Baseball Hall of Fame: 1992

Koosman turned in another strong showing (17-9 with a 2.28 ERA) and provided some important clutch pitching down the stretch of the pennant race. But Seaver was magnificent from start to finish, ending the year with a 25-7 record and a 2.21 earned run average.

At age 24, Seaver had already won 57 big league games on his way to 311 victories in a 20-year pitching career. He would lead the league in victories 3 times and in ERA 3 times, and strike out 3,640 batters to rank sixth all time, leading the league in strikeouts 5 times.

As the acknowledged best pitcher in baseball to close out a decade of great pitching, Seaver represented the last of a standard of excellence that was so prevalent among the best major league players of the 1960s.

179

Honorable Mention

60 More Players from the 1960s Whose Performances Deserve Recognition

60 From The '60s

Bob Allison, Minnesota Twins outfielder, hit 256 home runs in a 13-year career. Between 1961 and 1964, he averaged 31 home runs and 96 RBIs per season.

Felipe Alou, outfielder for the San Francisco Giants and Milwaukee Braves, led the National League in hits in 1966 (218) and 1968 (210). He hit .286 over a 17-year career.

Matty Alou, outfielder for the San Francisco Giants and Pittsburgh Pirates during the 1960s, led the National League in hitting in 1966 with a .342 average. With outstanding speed and bat control, he hit .307 over the course of his 15-year career.

Bob Allison   Felipe Alou   Lew Burdette

Max Alvis, Cleveland Indians third baseman, had a promising career derailed when he contracted spinal meningitis in 1964 and never had quite the same strength afterward. Always a solid defender, his best season was 1963 when he hit .274 with 22 home runs.

Luis Arroyo, New York Yankees pitcher, was a sub-.500 pitcher until he became a relief specialist. In 1961, Arroyo led the majors in appearances (65), games finished (59) and saves (29), while going 15-5 with a 2.19 ERA.

60 From The '60s

Richie Ashburn, a Hall of Fame outfielder for the Philadelphia Phillies, closed out his distinguished career in 1960-1962 with the Chicago Cubs and New York Mets. The 2-time National League batting champion hit .306 for the Mets in 1962.

Jim Bouton, New York Yankees pitcher, was a big winner for the Yankees in 1963 (21-7) and 1964 (18-13). His tell-all best-seller about that period, *Ball Four*, is still in print.

Lew Burdette pitched for 5 different teams during the 1960s after 12 years as a starter for the Milwaukee Braves. Burdette won 203 games over 18 seasons, winning 20 and 21, respectively, in 1958 and 1959.

Richie Ashburn   Rocky Colavito   Tommy Davis

Norm Cash, Detroit Tigers first baseman, had the highest single-season batting average in the 1960s with .361 in 1961. Over a 17-year career, Cash hit .271 with 377 home runs.

Rocky Colavito played outfield for 6 different teams during the 1960s. Colavito hit 45 home runs with 140 RBIs for Detroit in 1961, and led the American League with 108 RBIs as a member of the Cleveland Indians in 1965.

Mike Cuellar pitched for 4 teams during the 1960s, winning 16 games for the Houston Astros in 1967 and 23 games for the Baltimore Orioles in 1969. Cuellar went on to win 185 games in a 15-year career, including 4 seasons with 20 or more wins.

60 From The '60s

Tommy Davis played for 5 teams during the 1960s. As a Los Angeles Dodgers outfielder, Davis led the National League in hitting in 1962 (.346) and 1963 (.326). He led the major leagues in hits (230) and RBIs (153) in 1962.

Don Demeter played outfield for 5 teams during the 1960s. His best year was 1962 when he hit .307 for the Philadelphia Phillies with 29 home runs and 107 RBIs.

Dick Donovan pitched for 3 teams during the 1960s. As a starter for the Washington Senators, Donovan's 2.40 ERA led the American League in 1961. In 1962, he went 20-10 for the Cleveland Indians.

Don Demeter   Dick Donovan   Dick Ellsworth

Moe Drabowsky pitched for 5 different teams during the 1960s. As a member of the Baltimore Orioles bullpen, Drabowsky won the first game of the 1965 World Series by pitching 6.2 innings of hitless relief against the Los Angeles Dodgers, striking out 11 batters.

Dick Ellsworth pitched for 5 different teams during the 1960s. As a member of the Chicago Cubs, he accomplished the rare distinction of going from a 20-game loser in 1962 (9-20) to a 20-game winner the next year (22-10). He won 115 games over a 13-year career.

Eddie Fisher pitched for 5 different teams during the 1960s. Fisher won 15 games in relief for the Chicago White Sox in 1965, and saved 24 more. He led the American League in appearances in both 1965 and 1966.

Tito Francona played for 5 different teams during the 1960s. As a Cleveland Indians outfielder-first baseman, Francona hit .300 or better twice and led the American League in doubles with 36 in 1960.

Eddie Fisher   Tito Francona   "Mudcat" Grant

Bill Freehan, Detroit Tigers catcher, was a 5-time Gold Glove winner who hit .300 in 1962. He hit 25 home runs with 84 RBIs during the Tigers' championship season of 1968.

Bob Friend, Pittsburgh Pirates pitcher, won 18 games twice for the Bucs during the 1960s. He won 197 games over a 16-year career, 191 with Pittsburgh.

Jim Gentile played for 4 different teams during the 1960s. In 1961, as the Baltimore Orioles first baseman, Gentile had his best season, hitting .302 with 46 home runs and 141 RBIs.

Jim "Mudcat" Grant pitched for 5 different teams during the 1960s. He was a 15-game winner for the Cleveland Indians in 1961 and was the ace of the 1965 pennant-winning Minnesota Twins with a 21-7 record. Grant won 145 games over a 14-year career.

60 From The '60s

Ray Herbert pitched for 3 different teams during the 1960s. As a starter for the Chicago White Sox, Herbert won 20 games in 1962. He led the league in shutouts with 7 in 1963, going 13-10 that year for the White Sox.

Willie Horton, Detroit Tigers outfielder, hit 325 home runs over an 18-year career, the first 15 with the Tigers. His best overall year was 1968, when Horton hit .285 with 36 home runs and 85 RBIs. Horton drove in over 100 RBIs in a season 3 times, the last at age 36 for the Seattle Mariners … 106 RBIs in his next-to-last season.

Elston Howard, Yankee catcher and 1963 American League MVP, was a dependable, productive Gold Glove catcher for some great Yankee teams. He probably should have his own page in this recollection, but weren't there enough Yankees already?

Ray Herbert   Elston Howard   Larry Jackson

Ken Hubbs, Chicago Cubs second baseman, played only 2 full seasons before losing his life in a plane crash. The National League Rookie of the Year in 1962, he provided outstanding defense for the middle of the Cubs' infield, at one point going 78 consecutive games and 418 chances without making an error.

Jim "Catfish" Hunter, Hall of Fame pitcher for Kansas City-Oakland Athletics in the 1960s, came up with the A's in 1965. Though he was only 55-64 for some lackluster Athletics teams in the mid-to-late 60s, Hunter showed flashes of the kind of pitching brilliance that ultimately took him to Cooperstown, including a perfect game on May 8, 1968 against the Minnesota Twins.

60 From The '60s

Larry Jackson pitched for 3 teams in the 1960s. A workhorse who averaged 259 innings per season during the 1960s, Jackson led the majors in victories with 24 for the Chicago Cubs in 1964. Over a 14-year career, he won 194 games.

Joey Jay, Cincinnati Reds starting pitcher, came out of nowhere to lead the National League in wins in 1961 (with 21 – tying Warren Spahn) and followed with another 21-victory campaign in 1962. He lost 18 games for the Reds in 1963, and slipped back into obscurity, going 99-91 over a 13-year career.

Ferguson Jenkins, Hall of Fame pitcher, played for the Philadelphia Phillies and Chicago Cubs during the 1960s. Jenkins won 20 or more for the Cubs in 1967, 1968 and 1969, on the way to a total of 7 seasons with 20 or more victories and a career that included 284 wins and a Cy Young award (1971).

Tommy John, Chicago White Sox pitcher, started the decade with the Cleveland Indians and found little success there (2-11 over 2 seasons). With the White Sox, John became an outstanding starter, leading the majors in shutouts in both 1966 and 1967. His best years were still nearly a decade away, with a career that spanned 26 seasons and produced 288 victories.

Bobby Knoop, California Angels second baseman, was a great glove man who hit only .236 over a 9-season career. But in an era of great defensive second basemen, Knoop was probably the American League's best. He won 3 consecutive Gold Gloves starting in 1966, and that year led the American League in double plays with 135.

Jerry Koosman, New York Mets pitcher, was as good if not better than teammate Tom Seaver in the late 1960s. He was almost as instrumental in the rise of the Mets, winning 19 games in 1968 and 17 games (plus 2 World Series victories) in 1969. Koosman was a 20-game winner for the Mets in 1976 and for the Minnesota

Twins in 1979 on the way to a career victory total of 222 games over 19 seasons.

Ed Kranepool, New York Mets first baseman, was the poster child for the frustrations that were the early Mets. A fine player with a miserable team, Kranepool played 18 seasons for the Mets, hitting .261 lifetime with a season high of .323 in 1975.

Frank Lary pitched for 4 different teams during the 1960s. His best season was in 1961 as a Detroit Tiger, when he went 23-9 with a 3.24 ERA and led the majors in complete games with 22. Lary pitched for 12 seasons and won a total of 128 games, 123 for the Tigers.

Frank Lary   Vern Law   Jerry Lumpe

Vern Law, Pittsburgh Pirates pitcher, won the Cy Young award in 1960 with a 20-9 record and 3.08 ERA. He led the majors in complete games with 18 that year. Law won 162 games in 16 seasons, all with the Pirates.

Mickey Lolich, Detroit Tigers pitcher, won 3 games in the 1968 World Series as the Tigers took the series 4-3 over the St. Louis Cardinals. Lolich won 17 games that season and 19 the next on the way to a career victory total of 217 over 16 years, 13 with the Tigers.

Jim Lonborg, Boston Red Sox pitcher, won the American League Cy Young award in 1967 with a 22-9 record and a league-leading

246 strikeouts. Over a career that spanned 15 seasons and 3 teams, Lonborg won 157 games.

Jerry Lumpe played second base for the Kansas City Athletics and Detroit Tigers during the 1960s. His best season was 1962, when he hit .301 and drove in 83 runs. Over his 12-season career, Lumpe hit .268.

Jim Maloney, Cincinnati Reds pitcher, was the team's top starter from 1963 through 1968, a 20-game winner twice in that period (23-7 in 1963 and 20-9 in 1965) and never won fewer than 15. He also averaged 212 strikeouts per year during that period.

Jim Maloney   Eddie Mathews   Albie Pearson

Eddie Mathews, Hall of Fame third baseman for the Milwaukee Braves, hit 512 home runs over his 17-year career, twice leading the National League in round-trippers. While his most productive seasons came in the 1950s, Mathews bat was still lethal into the 1960s, averaging 29 home runs and 93 RBIs per season from 1960 to 1965.

Lindy McDaniel pitched for 4 teams during the 1960s. One of the most underrated pitchers of his era, McDaniel led the National League in saves 3 times, collecting 141 victories and 172 saves over his 21-season career.

60 From The '60s

Dave McNally, Baltimore Orioles pitcher, won 90 games for Baltimore during the 1960s, including a 22-10 record in 1968 and 20-7 in 1969. He won 20 or more games 4 times in his 14-season career, with a career total of 184 victories.

Joe Morgan, Hall of Fame second baseman, put together his best seasons as a member of the Cincinnati Reds in the 1970s, but also had some fine seasons for Houston in the late 1960s prior to being traded to the Big Red Machine.

Jim Palmer, Hall of Fame Baltimore Orioles pitcher, defeated Sandy Koufax 6-0 as part of a sweep over the Los Angeles Dodgers in the 1966 World Series, making him the last pitcher to defeat Koufax. The 20-year-old Palmer was the youngest man ever to pitch a World Series shutout. Palmer won 268 games over his 19-year career, all with Baltimore.

Albie Pearson, Los Angeles Angels outfielder, was the team's first "star," leading the American League by scoring 115 runs in 1962. He hit .275 in 6 years with the Angels.

Tony Perez, Hall of Fame Cincinnati Reds infielder, had a long and productive career that began in the 1960s and continued until 1986. From 1967 through 1969, he was a mainstay already in the Cincinnati offense, hitting .289 over that period and averaging 27 home runs and 105 RBIs per season. For his career, Perez had 379 home runs and over 1,652 RBIs, good for tenth place all-time among right-handed batters.

Rico Petrocelli, Boston Red Sox shortstop, set the American League record for home runs by a shortstop when he hit 40 in 1969. In 1970, he drove in 103 runs for the Red Sox. Over his 13-year career, all with Boston, Petrocelli hit 210 home runs.

Johnny Podres, Los Angeles Dodgers pitcher, was the team's number 3 starter in the early 1960s after Sandy Koufax and Don

Drysdale. His best season was 1961 when he went 18-5. Podres won 148 in a career that lasted 15 seasons, 13 with the Dodgers.

Pedro Ramos pitched for 6 teams during the 1960s. After losing an average of 19 games per year with the Washington Senators/Minnesota Twins, Ramos struggled as a sub-.500 starter-reliever for the Cleveland Indians for the next 3 years. When he was traded to the New York Yankees, Ramos became their bullpen ace and saved 32 games over the next 2 years for a declining Yankees team. Essentially, Pete Ramos was talented enough to lose a lot of games … and deserved better.

Pedro Ramos   Jack Sanford   Norm Siebern

Jack Sanford pitched for 3 different teams in the 1960s. His best year came in 1962 with the San Francisco Giants, as Sanford posted a 24-7 record to lead the staff. He won 137 games over his 12-year career.

Chris Short, Philadelphia Phillies pitcher, was a bellwether for the Phillies staff in the late 1960s, winning 20 games in 1966 and 19 games in 1968. From 1964 through 1968, his earned run average was 2.82. Short won 135 games in 15 seasons, all but one with Philadelphia.

Norm Siebern, Kansas City Athletics first baseman, was acquired by the A's in the deal that sent Roger Maris to the New York Yankees. Siebern was a dependable fixture at first base for Kansas City, averaging 19 home runs and 78 RBIs during his 4 seasons with the A's. His best year was 1962, when he hit .308 with 25 home runs and 117 RBIs.

Sonny Siebert, Cleveland Indians pitcher, was 16-8 for the Tribe in both 1965 and 1966, with earned run averages of 2.43 and 2.80 respectively. Siebert no-hit the Washington Senators on June 10, 1966. He was traded to the Boston Red Sox in 1969, and had 4 solid seasons as a Boston starter. Siebert posted 140 victories over a 12-season career.

Leon Wagner   Bill White   Earl Wilson

Rusty Staub played outfield and first base for the Houston Astros and Montreal Expos. Staub was a consistent, though not overpowering, hitter. His best year for the Astros was 1967 when he hit .333 and led the majors with 44 doubles. Traded to Montreal in 1969, Staub hit .302 for the Expos that year. He was a .279 lifetime hitter over a 23-year career, collecting 2,716 hits.

Leon Wagner played outfield for 5 teams in the 1960s. He twice had 100-RBI seasons: 107 (with 37 home runs) for the Los Angeles Angels in 1962, and 100 (with 31 home runs) for the Cleveland Indians in 1964. Over a 12-season career, mostly with the Angels and Indians, Wagner hit .272 with 211 home runs.

Bill White played first base for the St. Louis Cardinals and Philadelphia Phillies during the 1960s. He hit .286 over 13 seasons and collected 7 Gold Gloves. His best year was 1963, when White hit .304 with 27 home runs and 109 RBIs for the Cardinals.

Ted Williams, Hall of Fame Boston Red Sox outfielder, played only one year in the 1960s, and made it memorable. Perhaps the greatest left-handed hitter of all time (With apologies to Mr. Ruth, Mr. Cobb and Mr. Musial), Williams hit his home run number 500 in June of 1960 and ended his career with a home run in his last at-bat. Now that's going out with style.

Don Wilson, Houston Astros pitcher, was talented enough to be a consistent winner on a losing club. He pitched 2 no-hitters for the Astros, and won 103 games in eight full seasons with Houston.

Earl Wilson pitched for the Boston Red Sox and Detroit Tigers in the 1960s. The big right-hander won 52 games for the Red Sox from 1962 to 1966. He had his best years with the Tigers, leading the American League with 22 victories in 1967 (tied with Boston's Jim Lonborg). Wilson won 121 games altogether over his 11-year major league career.

About the Author

Carroll Conklin combines a life-long passion for baseball with a three-decade career as a professional writer.

A graduate of Ashland University and Bowling Green State University, Carroll has spent more than 20 years as an advertising copywriter and marketing strategist. He has taught copywriting and brand theory at The Ohio State University and the Columbus College of Art & Design.

A prolific author, Carroll has also written books on topics ranging from marketing management to fear elimination.

He preaches the "gospel" of the 1960s as baseball's real golden age at www.1960sBaseball.com.

CPSIA information can be obtained
at www.ICGtesting.com
Printed in the USA
BVHW071230201218
536083BV00015B/640/P